Reading Dave Carbonell is like sitting down with an ol
and healthy dose of humor puts you at ease and makes
digest. Dave knows something about anxiety that you
airborne again. Anxiety feels big and scary but it plays the same tricks over and over
again. Why should you trust Dave? Because he successfully treats people like you and
me every day, both on the ground and in the air. If you have a fear of flying, do yourself
a favor. Pick up this book, do the work, and start planning your next adventure!

—*Kristin E. Cummings, LCSW,*
author and creator of the The Adventures of Anxiety Girl

This workbook is the essential tool you need to conquer your fear of
flying. David Carbonell has successfully treated hundreds of people
with this problem. Get his book and earn your wings!

—*Jennifer Shannon, LMFT, cofounder of the Santa Rosa Center for Cognitive*
Behavioral Therapy and author of Don't Feed The Monkey Mind, The Anxiety
Survival Guide for Teens, *and* The Shyness and Social Anxiety Workbook for Teens

Rather than spending too much time explaining how and why flying is safe, Dr.
Carbonell, drawing on his years of experience, gets right to the heart of the matter
in what's needed to overcome aviophobia. In his clear and delightfully engaging
workbook, he educates in a manner that even the most doubtful of the fearful
will very likely find inspiring. Thank you, Dr. C, for sharing your wisdom and
strategies in this invaluable resource for fearful fliers and those who help them!

—*Vikki L. Brown, Ed. D., licensed psychologist, fear of flying*
specialist, faculty member in psychology, Harvard Medical School/
Cambridge Health Alliance, Cambridge, Massachusetts

Dave has once again applied his tried and true techniques for defeating the Panic
Trick to an area in which he has an amazing amount of experience. This book
is a step-by-step manual to ultimately challenge aviophobia and take a flight.
Or, it will be the step that you need to prepare to work with a professional who
will get you over the flying hurdle. Read this book—the skies are calling.

—*Patrick B. McGrath, Ph.D., clinical director at the Center for Anxiety*
and OCD at Alexian Brothers Behavioral Health Hospital, author of
The OCD Answer Book *and* Don't Try Harder, Try Different

Dr. Carbonell's *Fear of Flying Workbook* is superb and a must-read for the fearful flier. The workbook explains the basis of the fear from both psychological and neurological perspectives but in accessible language. Equally important, Dr. Carbonell provides techniques and exercises enshrined in his "Rules of Opposites," and he distinguishes danger from discomfort. What makes this book excellent is the inclusion of non-flying anecdotes/examples anyone can relate to. A tad of levity in Dr. Carbonell's delivery also makes it easier to digest a subject likely to invoke anxiety for the fearful flier.

—Douglas Boyd, Ph.D., licensed pilot, FAA safety team representative,
owner of Flying Phobia Help in Houston, Texas

Just as he did in *Panic Attacks Workbook*, Dave has written about difficult concepts in a way that is readable, approachable, and gives individuals real hope, as well as concrete strategies they can use as they learn to relate differently to their fears around flying. A must read for any fearful flier!

—Stephnie Thomas, LCPC, Associate and Fear of Flying Specialist,
The Anxiety & Stress Disorders Institute, Towson, MD

Fear of Flying WORKBOOK

Overcome Your Anticipatory Anxiety and Develop Skills for Flying with Confidence

David Carbonell, PhD

Ulysses Press

Published in the U.S. by
Ulysses Press
P.O. Box 3440
Berkeley, CA 94703
www.ulyssespress.com

ISBN: 978-1-61243-719-4
Library of Congress Control Number: 2017937989

Printed in the United States by United Graphics Inc.
10 9 8 7 6 5 4 3 2 1

Acquisitions editor: Bridget Thoreson
Managing editor: Claire Chun
Editor: Renee Rutledge
Proofreader: Shayna Keyles
Front cover and interior design: what!design @ whatweb.com
Layout: Jake Flaherty

Distributed by Publishers Group West

To my wife Ellen and my son Adam, who bore the burden of a writer in the house with grace and patience. Thanks for the support, the edits, and the snacks!

Contents

....

Foreword

. . . .

When I was seven years old, my mother, step-father, and I took a typical city dwellers' vacation: We went to a dude ranch. I recall only three things about that trip, two of which were painful and one that was a triumph:

- my beloved stuffed rabbit, Roy, got lost somewhere in transit;

- a horse that I rode at the ranch bucked and left me with blacks and blues that turned astounding shades of purple, yellow, and green; and

- my mother, terrified of flying, clutched my hand the entire flight from New York to Denver.

Or at least that's how I recall it. The triumph? I felt very grown up as I gently held my mother's hand, expressed soothing words to her, and attempted to distract her from her dread.

What happened as a result of this experience? Well, I didn't develop a fear of flying, either from genetic predisposition or the "modeling" of fear that my mother displayed. On reflection now, it may have contributed to my choice of future career as a performance and clinical psychologist: It was pretty exciting and satisfying to feel like I was being helpful!

Over time, my mother became much more adept at flying—a very good thing, since she loved travel and we had a number of terrific trips on both sides of the Atlantic.

If the same scenario of flying with my frightened mother happened today, after I had read David Carbonell's *Fear of Flying Workbook*, I might approach the whole situation quite differently. I might understand just how scared she was. I would know some of the usual platitudes and advice—the ones that don't help. Most importantly, I could support her in speaking and acting in ways that could actually help: I could help her work with her fear rather than trying to get her to stop feeling afraid.

But enough about my mother (and me). If you're afraid of flying, yet have gotten yourself to pick up this book and read even these few seemingly harmless paragraphs, let me congratulate you and tell you that you are in for a treat. Get ready for a wonderful opportunity to be guided by a thoroughly caring, accepting, reassuring voice of wisdom and knowledge. In an utterly conversational tone and with respect for your struggles, Dr. David Carbonell gets inside your head—and maybe more importantly, gives you permission to get inside your own head. He'll help you understand and really deal with the nuances of fear, embracing the tone of Franklin Roosevelt's famous "we have nothing to fear but fear itself." Through analogy and example, Dr. Carbonell demonstrates a perceptive knowledge of anxiety, which feeds—even thrives!—on our attempts to contain, curb, and control it.

Spoiler alert: Dr. Carbonell won't make it easy for you. He'll expect you to do your own work. This is *your* fear of flying, after all. But he'll give you a path—a flight path, if you will—that will ultimately help you board a plane, feel the fear, observe and learn more about yourself, and get through it to your destination.

This workbook is about a specific fear. It's also broader than that, reminding us that this is how we can best move forward through the journey of life: with awareness and appreciation, recognition of complexities, by learning and finding ways of living through challenges. Travel well!

—Kate F. Hays, Ph.D.

Kate F. Hays, Ph.D., offers sport, performance, and clinical psychology consultation through her Toronto practice, The Performing Edge. She is a past president of the Society for Sport, Exercise & Performance Psychology (American Psychological Association's division 47) and has published five books on performance psychology as well as on exercise and mental health.

Introduction

....

You can overcome the fear of flying. But right now, you probably feel nervous just scanning this book. That's okay. I think anyone who's ever attended my fearful flier workshops felt nervous, even panicky, when they got the e-mail reminding them the group was about to start. Just thinking about it could make their hearts race, palms sweat, chests tighten, and breathing become labored and uncomfortable. Then all the scary thoughts they usually have about flying would flood their mind. They'd start having nervous thoughts about being the most frightened person in the group, and think they should back out.

Don't be fooled by those thoughts. If you're afraid of flying and start thinking of flying for any reason, you'll probably experience some fear. I'm going to help you with that. For now, if you find yourself struggling against that fear, turn your attention back to these words for a few minutes without trying to control what you feel: You don't have to feel calm to read—you can let that develop over time.

In this book, I'll show you an approach to aviophobia, the fear of flying, that will help you start flying again if you've stopped entirely. Or, if you still fly, but with increasing dread and difficulty, you'll be able to approach flying in a new way, one that gradually relieves and diminishes the anxiety you feel before and during each flight. As a clinical psychologist who has specialized in helping people overcome all kinds of fears and phobias since 1990, my methods combine elements of cognitive behavioral therapy (CBT) with a variety of acceptance-based methods, principally derived from acceptance and commitment therapy (ACT). I've written books about various aspects of anxiety, have maintained a popular self-help website at AnxietyCoach.com since 2000, and offered training about fears and phobias to thousands of professional therapists in the US and abroad.

I'm confident you can take some big steps in the next 30 days. It may be hard for you to believe that this problem can be overcome, or that you can take your first practice flight so soon. This is a very common reaction. However, I know it's true because I've seen many people do it.

When I first started offering my workshop for fearful fliers in 1993, the groups met once a week for four weeks, and then we'd take a flight together. In the last few years, I've conducted the workshop in a single weekend, with the flight on a Sunday afternoon. Both ways have been very effective, and these groups have included a lot of people who hadn't flown for 10 years or more. More than 600 people have attended the workshops, and all but five of them have taken the flights. So, taking one month to started addressing your fear is a reasonable timeframe. Take more time if you choose to. It's not a race.

One out of every six people fears flying. It is a solvable problem, and yet, people often have a lot of trouble solving it. They often struggle in fear and frustration for years. The reason people have so much trouble overcoming this problem isn't because it's so difficult, nor because these people are defective. It's because the Panic Trick fools them into opposing their fear with methods that they hope will help, but that actually make their fear stronger and more durable. I'm going to help you discover how this works, how it may have prevented you from solving the problem of fear, and above all, how you can solve it and travel as you see fit. For now, I'll just say that this fear is a counterintuitive problem, and when you use intuitive responses with a counterintuitive problem, that makes it worse rather than better. In this book, I'll help you develop better responses.

I'm going to assume that you have the same goal as all the fearful fliers I've worked with; namely, you want to be able to fly on commercial airlines whenever it serves your purposes. You want to be a passenger. This is a book for people who want to be passengers.

Whether you want to overcome this fear in order to fly for business purposes, or because you're at a point in life when you have the time and money to travel and you want to see more of the world, or because you're preparing for college and don't want to limit your options to nearby schools, it's all doable.

I'll show you how to treat this problem in ways that actually do make it more manageable. You'll learn how to use the same techniques we use in my fearful flier workshop. This will enable you to join the ranks of former flight-phobics who can now travel by airplane whenever they wish.

Sound scary? Of course it does! That's because you're afraid of flying. If you were afraid of dogs (or spiders), and I was writing about approaching dogs (or spiders), you'd feel afraid as well. That's what this book is for. Take it a step at a time, and I think you'll find that you'll regain the ability to fly and travel freely.

A note about using this book: I'm going to periodically ask you to answer questions, try an experiment, or engage in some task before you continue reading. Some readers prefer to read first and do the exercises later. Others will do the exercises as they come to them, in the order I present. Both methods are okay. But there are two good reasons to do each exercise or task as soon as you reach it in the book, rather than putting it off.

The first reason is that it's very important to *do the exercises*. And you're more likely to do them all if you simply go ahead and do each one as you come to them, rather than putting them off or waiting for a "better time." You don't have to do it this way; you can wait if you want, but some of the people who postpone the exercises will probably not get back to them. And if you read the book but don't do the exercises, you probably won't get much out of it. Therefore, you can increase your chances of a good outcome by responding to each exercise as it arises.

The second reason is that I'm going to mention common answers and reactions to the questions and experiments, and it will be more useful for you to record your own answers before you read the answers of other people. So, you can do it either way, but my suggestion is to just tackle each question and exercise when you come to it.

Before we begin, here are three definitions you might find useful.

Fear: a strong expectation of future danger, which usually produces anxiety.

Anxiety: an emotion characterized by feelings of tension, worried thoughts, and physical changes, like increased blood pressure.

Phobia: a fear of a specific situation, object, activity, or other cue that is disproportionate to the probability of potential harm it contains, accompanied by a persistent pattern of avoidance and self-protective responses.

Ready to get started? You may be having the thought that you should wait for a better time, when you feel less nervous. Don't be fooled by that thought! Postponing will actually prolong the problem, while engaging with it can lead to a solution. If you're afraid of flying, thinking and reading about flying will make you nervous at first. If you're going to solve this problem, you'll feel some fear along the way. Trying not to be afraid is how you remain phobic, not how you overcome it. You will feel some fear as you read this and work on it, and that will be okay. In fact, working with that fear, rather than against it, is how you will overcome this problem and regain your freedom to fly whenever and wherever it meets your needs.

Good luck with the program. If you ever see me at the airport, be sure to say hello!

CHAPTER 1

What Do You Fear About Flying?

....

Think back to a time when you were on board an airplane waiting for takeoff, and you felt very afraid. Pretend I could have spoken to you at that moment and that you were willing to talk briefly with me. Let's suppose I asked you, "What do you fear will happen to you on this flight?" How would you have answered me at that moment?

Don't tell me what you think now. Tell me what you feared then, in the moments before take-off. Don't try to dress up your fear to make it seem more realistic or reasonable. No one else has to see your answer if you don't want them to. Just state, simply and concretely, what you feared was going to happen to you when you flew on that airplane, regardless of how realistic or unrealistic that fear seems to you right now.

People are often a little vague in their first answers. They often say things like "doom" and "losing control" and "being trapped." So be as specific as you can. If you feared doom, what form did you think that doom would take, and what would it do to you? If you feared losing control, what out-of-control things did you think you might do? If you feared being trapped, what did you fear would happen to you in that trap?

_____

_____

_____

Two Types of Feared Outcomes

The previous question is the first one I ask fearful fliers. They typically answer with one of two very different feared outcomes.

The **Type 1 feared outcome** is about the plane crashing and killing the passengers. In my experience, about one third of fearful fliers report this feared outcome. They're not afraid of flying, they're afraid of crashing, at least as they first report it.

They often go on to explain that they're less afraid of death itself than they are of the fear and stress they imagine they would experience while the plane is about to crash. They think about that a lot, repeatedly imagining what they think it would be like. They even think about how unfair it would be, how irritated they would become, if they went through all the trouble to overcome their fears just to die in a plane crash and never even get an apology from all the friends and family who mocked their fears!

People who fear crashing spend a lot of time anticipating a doomed flight and feeling afraid as they experience the anticipation. They are literally afraid of feeling afraid.

Most members of the public who are not afraid of flying tend to believe that crashing is what all fearful fliers fear. It usually doesn't occur to them that the fear could be anything other than crashing and dying. However, this is not the fear of the majority of fearful fliers. Again, only about one third of the participants in my workshop have reported this Type 1 feared outcome over the years, and this is roughly the percentage reported by past studies of fear of flying.

The **Type 2 feared outcome** is quite different and doesn't have anything to do with airplane safety. People with this fear worry that they will become so afraid during the flight that they'll suffer some terrible consequence as a result of their fear. They think of the airplane not as a vehicle that will rapidly take them to their destination, but as some kind of trap from which escape is impossible. They're afraid of how they imagine the confinement in the airplane will affect them. This kind of fear is very similar to claustrophobia, a fear of being confined in a small space without means of escape.

A person with claustrophobia might become very afraid, for instance, if they have to get an MRI scan done on some part of their body. This generally requires that they lie down in a dark, closed tube. There isn't anything in the MRI that will hurt them, and all they have to do is lie there in the same posture they would use to sleep. However, if they have claustrophobia, they might find it very difficult to agree to this test because they expect to feel very afraid in there. If you ask a claustrophobic person what they fear will happen to them in the MRI tube, they'll probably have a hard time answering that question, maybe saying that they just "can't stand it" and hate and fear the confinement. If you ask more questions, you might discover that this person experiences thoughts and images of losing control—yelling, crying, trying to force their way out of the tube, and so on. More discussion might reveal that they also fear and dread the shame and humiliation they expect to experience in response to acting this way. Some people who experience claustrophobia have fearful thoughts of becoming so afraid that they lose their mind and never get it back. This is very similar to the Type 2 feared outcome.

Again, people with this fear aren't afraid of flying or crashing. They have a different, dual fear. They expect to feel nervous and afraid because they think of the airplane as a trap. They think of themselves as trapped on the airplane for however long the flight lasts, without the ability to leave. And, they're afraid that the nervousness and fear they experience in this trapped circumstance will overwhelm and overpower them, either causing them physical harm or leading them to act in ways that bring terrible consequences.

Some worry that they will suffer a heart attack, stroke, or some other physical calamity in response to feeling so afraid. They worry that they will literally be "scared to death."

Others worry that they will become so afraid as to lose control of themselves and charge the cockpit, or try to open a door or break a window, or start crying and screaming uncontrollably, or loudly demanding to be allowed off the plane immediately. People with this type of fear usually imagine it ending with the crew and passengers overpowering them, restraining them with handcuffs, duct tape, ropes, or whatever else may be available, and returning to the airport to turn them over to the authorities, all of which gets broadcast on the local news for all their family and friends and neighbors to see.

Either way, they fear that they will never be themselves again, even if they survive. Just like people with Type 1 fear, they, too, are literally afraid of feeling afraid.

The fact that most people who don't fear flying assume that the fear is all about crashing makes it harder for people with Type 2 fears, because it means that it will be harder for others to understand them. I see this happen all the time with fearful fliers when we board the airplane for our flight and I mention to the flight attendant who's greeting the passengers that we're a fearful fliers class. They're always very supportive and encouraging, but they frequently assume that our group is all afraid of crashing. They point out how good the pilot is and promise that the flight will be very safe. This doesn't at all reassure people with Type 2 fears because they're not really worried about airline safety, and it often leaves them feeling more awkward about what they do fear.

Preexisting Fears

While the great majority of fearful fliers identify either crashing or losing control of themselves as their fear, people can bring other preexisting fears on board with them. Someone who fears heights often has a hard time on airplanes. Someone with obsessive fears about food, who is suspicious of food prepared by others, is likely to be worried about having an adequate supply of "safe" food, especially on international flights. Someone with a fear of using public bathrooms is probably going to experience that fear on board the plane. People who fear nausea and vomiting are likely to worry about becoming sick on the plane. People who fear strangers, or not being sufficiently close to a hospital in case of an emergency, or being too far from home, will similarly experience those fears on board the plane.

What makes it possible to have so many different fears on board an airplane? It's because the fear doesn't reside in the airplane itself. The fear resides in our reaction to the airplane. This is why some people will sleep or do crossword puzzles, while others will have a panic attack. They're all on the same plane, having different reactions. It's the fear, not the flying, that matters.

While the details of the fears will vary, the same approach used in this book to overcome the fear of fear can be applied to these other types of fears as well.

Working with Your Fear

Now that you've considered what you fear, I have another question to ask you.

Why do you want to fly even though you are so afraid of flying?

_____

_____

_____

When I ask fearful fliers this question, they usually cite the advantages of flying, pointing out, for instance, that flying from Chicago to the West Coast will save them several days of driving, giving them more time to enjoy their vacation with the family. They'll point out that there are many parts of the world that are so distant that it's hardly practical to go by ship. Cruises to Europe, for instance, can take seven days or more, while many flights take that many hours.

They'll sometimes answer by referencing the pressures they feel from their family to travel. They explain that a spouse is really tired of the limits this imposes on their vacations, or that their extended family is planning a big trip abroad. Sometimes they explain that their children will soon be old enough to ask for a trip to Disneyland, and they don't know how to answer that request. They often express the desire that their children grow up without becoming afraid of flying.

Others point to the need to travel for their jobs and careers. Sometimes a promotion, or a new job, requires air travel. Some people are just dissatisfied with the limits this fear imposes on their lives, and unwilling or unable to accept it.

But when you think about these reasons, there's something funny about them. If you don't want to fly because you figure it will kill you, or end up with you in jail, why would you want to make that trip in the first place? Is it really worth saving a few days of driving when the price is...death? Or prison? Insanity or disgrace?

When I ask people about this, they usually explain that they still want to fly because they know the fear is exaggerated, irrational, or illogical. They want to fly, not because they're willing to give up their life, freedom, or sanity so they can save a few days of driving. They want to fly, despite these fears, because they recognize that their fears are unrealistic in the extreme! That's why they want their children to grow up without this fear, because it doesn't help you lead a safer or better life in any way. It limits your freedom but doesn't make you more safe or give you any advantages in return.

That makes sense. I've worked with thousands of people who wanted to overcome fears of all kinds, yet no one has ever come to me because they wanted to overcome a fear of jumping into the lion cage at the zoo. That would be dangerous! People generally only want to overcome fears, like the fear of flying, when they recognize that the fear doesn't really protect them from danger. They want to overcome fears that restrict their freedom without providing any increased safety. Nobody wants to overcome fears that serve a useful purpose.

So, the people who come to me for help with fear of flying recognize that they have a fear that's irrational, or unrealistic, or excessive, or whatever other adjective they use to describe it. They have a fear of fear, rather than of danger. The fear is the problem, not the flying. That's why they want to be able to fly again! And if you've read this far into this book on how to overcome the fear of flying, this is probably your motivation as well. Working with the fear of fear is the key to overcoming the fear of flying.

It's true that some fearful fliers get so unhappy with the pressure they feel from others to overcome this fear that they get defensive about it and will actually argue with others to justify their fears. Maybe you've occasionally found yourself in that uncomfortable position. But that's more a response to the aggravation of being pressured by others than it is a judgment about flying. If you have this fear and also want to overcome it, it's probably because you recognize that the risk is overstated.

The very fact that you want to overcome the fear of flying, the fact that you want to fly anyway, tells us something important about the fear and points to the way out of this phobia. We'll take a closer look at this in the next chapter.

CHAPTER 2

What Kind of Fear Is This?

....

So, we're talking about a particular kind of fear, a fear you want to overcome. You're afraid of flying, and yet, you want to fly. Maybe you're afraid of crashing, or maybe you have a claustrophobic fear of losing control. But you want to fly despite your fear. You want to fly because you recognize the fears are exaggerated. Unfortunately, no matter how hard you've tried, you haven't been able to convince yourself that you'll be okay if you get on a plane. And that's so frustrating.

Let's back up and look at the big picture. Although we often assume that feeling afraid is a reliable sign of danger, it's often not true, and I'll explore this issue in the next chapter. For now, let's simply note that not all fears are created equal. Some give you a timely, accurate signal of danger and fulfill the evolutionary purpose of fear, which is to call your attention to a threat and fill you with the energy you need to run away or fight it off. This is the one that people sometimes think of as a rational fear. The other kind seems to fill you with fear to no useful purpose, when there isn't any actual danger, at least at the moment. That's the one people sometimes call irrational.

It's often unhelpful to label the fear of flying as irrational. It can get in the way of your progress. For one thing, the term "irrational" sounds kind of critical and insulting. For another, it's common for people who struggle with fear of flying to start thinking of *themselves* as irrational, rather than the fears. They take this exaggerated, unrealistic fear to mean that they're irrational people, rather than people who have some irrational fears, but who also function very well in most aspects of life. You don't have to be irrational to have an irrational fear! In fact, we all have some irrational fears.

Here's an example of an "irrational" fear shared by many. If you go to the 12th floor of most buildings in downtown Chicago (or most other large American cities) and go up one more floor, what floor do you come to?

You come to the 13th floor. But we call it the 14th floor, and mark it with signs as such.

Why do we do that? Because there are enough people in the general population who fear the number 13 that it will be harder to rent out offices and apartments if the floor is labeled that way. The building owner will have to charge less rent on that floor in order to fill the vacancies. Think of it—a building with a floor labeled 13 will earn less rent than an identical building that labels it 14!

So, don't get too troubled by the fact that you, too, have fears you recognize as exaggerated or irrational. It's a common part of life!

Signal Fear Versus False Alarm

The key difference between these two fears is not how they feel physically. The biological experience of these two different fears is very similar. The key difference is whether or not the fear gives you a reliable warning of present danger or not. Instead of calling them "rational" and "irrational," I'm going to use these terms:

A **signal fear** fills you with fear to call your attention to a current threat. This threat, if left unattended, could cause you serious harm. A signal fear alerts you to its presence and fills you with the energy you need to protect yourself.

A **false alarm** doesn't discriminate between safety and danger. It's like a dog that barks at everyone who comes near your house, not just the bad guys. It sounds an alarm whether danger is present or not. It's like a powerfully over-learned habit.

Let's think about a man who walks through a village and encounters a bunch of dogs. Some of them wag their tails as he approaches, while some bark. Some run loose through the village, while others are on leashes or behind fences. Some are large, and some are small. And there's one, roaming the streets freely, that growls viciously, with fur back and teeth bared.

If our man has a strong fear of dogs, a dog phobia, he's likely to feel afraid of all those dogs. Just seeing the dogs, including the friendly ones, the ones behind secure fences, maybe even the doggy in the window, is enough to bring on fear. That's what it is to have a phobia. This fear doesn't discriminate between the dogs that are likely to hurt you and the dogs that just want to be your friend. It's a false alarm. It doesn't really offer any useful guidance about how to live a safer life. It just tells you to be afraid and to avoid every dog in the world.

A person without a dog phobia would probably feel afraid as the dog that growls viciously approached, with fur back and teeth bared, but not feel especially afraid of the others. This is a signal fear. It discriminates between the dog that is likely to attack you and the dogs that probably won't. It offers a useful warning about how to be safer. It tells you to stay away from that growling dog, or you might get hurt. You can safely walk past the others, and pet them if you like.

These are two very different fears, even though they may feel the same. It's important to make the distinction. Now, back to the fear you have of flying: Is it a signal fear, or a false alarm?

If your fear is principally about crashing, a signal fear would only lead you to feel afraid when you're on a flight that's in danger of crashing. However, you could experience a false alarm simply by booking a flight, boarding a plane, flying through turbulent air, or even thinking of flying while you're driving to work, maybe because you heard a travel commercial or saw a plane overhead.

If what you fear is crashing, do you have a signal fear or a false alarm?

A signal fear gives you an accurate warning of current danger, while a false alarm does not. The best way to judge what kind of fear you have now is to look at how well it functioned in the past. So you can answer this question by reviewing how useful and accurate your fear has been in the past.

For the flights you feared would crash, did they tend to do that?	Y	N
Has it ever happened that, when you thought your flight would crash, it did?	Y	N
Have you feared flights that routinely arrived at your intended destination?	Y	N
Have you ever sat on a flight, full of fear of crashing, with strong physical sensations of fear and scary thoughts as well, and wondered why everyone else on the plane seemed to be unconcerned?	Y	N
Are you now in the habit of fearing a crash whenever you fly, or plan to fly?	Y	N
When you leave a plane before it departs out of fear of a crash, do you continue to expect that flight to crash?	Y	N
Does a flight have a decreased chance of crashing, in your mind, once you've gotten off the plane?	Y	N
Think of those times you got off a plane before takeoff, fearing it would crash. Did you later check to see if it crashed?	Y	N
Off all the planes you've gotten off before takeoff, have any of them crashed?	Y	N

If your fear accurately discriminated between the flights that crashed and the flights that landed safely, then you would have a signal fear. But you'd probably also have a highly paid job with the Federal Aviation Administration deciding which flights to cancel! Most people who fear crashing tend to suppose that whatever flight they take, that's the one that will crash, and if they cancel their ticket, that flight goes back onto the "safe" list. That's a false alarm. It just leads you to feel afraid whenever you fly, plan to fly, or think about flying. It doesn't discriminate between flights that are safe and flights that are dangerous, and it doesn't lead you to act in ways that make you safer. A false alarm can play over and over in your head like a broken record.

Maybe you think that, if there's any chance of dying in a crash, you should avoid the flight, even though your fear has never accurately predicted a crash, and you fear a crash every time you fly or think about it. That's still a false alarm. It doesn't help you discriminate between safe and unsafe flights; it just tells you to fear them all, regardless of the actual risk. And it tells you—screams at you might be more like it—to avoid flying, all while happily allowing you to engage in all kinds of daily activities that are far more dangerous than flying.

Even those people who identify crashing as their fear are really more afraid of becoming afraid, or feeling panicked, than they are of crashing. They have the same fear of fear as do people who fear losing control of themselves. We'll see some evidence for this in Chapter 6, when we look at how people respond to their fear and what they do in their efforts to solve this problem.

If your fear isn't so much crashing, but rather panicking on board the flight, losing control of yourself, and ending up in jail or a mental hospital, does your fear allow you to tell which flights this will happen on and which flights it won't? You can answer this question the same way, by considering your track record with this fear.

What's the most out-of-control thing you've done when you've had this fear?

_____

List some of the fears you've experienced about how you might behave, or misbehave, on board an aircraft.

_____

_____

_____

Which of these have you actually done?

_____

(I only gave you one line to answer that, but you probably didn't need even that much space.)

When you feared losing control of yourself on flights, did you actually do something disruptive or out of control?	**Y**	**N**
Has it ever happened, just because you feared losing control, that you lost control of yourself and did something disruptive?	**Y**	**N**
Have you feared losing control on flights and just sat there without disruption?	**Y**	**N**
Are you now in the habit of fearing losing control of yourself whenever you fly or plan to fly?	**Y**	**N**

When I asked you to write down the out-of-control things you've actually done on a flight, did your answer include phrases like "once, I almost" or "I came close to"? This is how the fear can trick you. I'm not asking about times you thought you came close to doing something, while simply sitting there doing nothing objectionable. I'm asking about what you actually *did*. Don't confuse your thoughts and feelings with your actions! If you owed a friend some money and kept thinking about repaying it without ever doing so, that would be little consolation to your friend! Actions count for something. Fearful thoughts and feelings, experienced as part of a phobia, not so much.

Did your answer start with the words "what if"? If so, you're telling me about something bad that you think you could do in the future, although you probably have never done that. Or, as many of my clients have said, "I haven't done that, *yet*." This isn't anything you've done, it's something you worry about doing. We'll take up this kind of anticipatory fear in Chapter 10.

With those points in mind, reconsider your answer to this question. Have you ever actually *done* anything disruptive on an airplane, something that brought you into conflict with the crew? _____

If you have a history of actual disruptive behavior, be sure to read about Group 2 (see page 20).

If you're like most people with a fear of flying, your history probably shows that your fear has no predictive power whatsoever, that it hasn't ever accurately predicted an outcome. If a person always fears that his flight will crash, or that he will go berserk on the flight and rush the cockpit, or get so afraid that he will "die of fright," but has never experienced the calamity he fears, that fear has a batting average of zero. If your stock broker had a batting average of zero in terms of picking stocks that would make money, you'd find another stockbroker. These are not predictions you want to be guided by.

Here's an exercise I've used on group practice flights. During the flight, I ask one of the participants, someone especially concerned with losing control of himself, to ring the attendant button and ask for a packet of sugar. Since none of the participants typically drink coffee during a flight, the participant usually protests that it's a stupid idea, and that the attendant would be annoyed, because he has no need for the sugar. Still, I persist in urging the passenger to ask for the unnecessary sugar.

I have a perfect record of failure on this! I've never persuaded anyone to request the sugar, although it would have been harmless if they had. But once it was clear that the passenger was not going to ask for the sugar, then I could have a useful conversation with him. I could point out that, if he was so reluctant to inconvenience the flight attendant with this silly request for sugar, how much less likely was he to storm the cockpit or try to open a door?

The best response to a false alarm is to allow yourself to feel afraid and not struggle in any way to protect yourself. This method is often referred to as desensitization, exposure, exposure and response prevention, and similar terms. It means, if you have a dog phobia, the way to overcome it is to spend a lot of time with dogs, let yourself feel afraid, and give the feelings time to subside. And if you're afraid of flying, flying is your dog. This recognition that your fear doesn't discriminate between safety and danger, that it's not a useful warning sign, is terribly important. It means that it's okay to feel afraid, in the same way that it's okay to feel tired or upset. The fear won't lead to some terrible event. It's discomfort, not danger. The fear of flying doesn't offer you any useful signal of actual danger. It may be uncomfortable and inconvenient to feel afraid, but all that's at stake is how you feel, temporarily.

Wouldn't it feel better to stop feeling afraid? Yes, absolutely! Then shouldn't you resist the false alarm and try to stop feeling and thinking that way? Absolutely not! If that were going to work, you wouldn't be reading this book now, you'd be calmly flying to Tahiti or Paris. This fear is a counterintuitive problem. It's understandable that your instinct is to oppose and resist it. But, as we'll see in Chapter 3 and elsewhere throughout this book, struggling against this fear usually leads you to feel worse rather than better. What you resist, persists.

Now it's time to assess more clearly the type of fear you have. There are four groups, and it's going to be very helpful for you to consider which group you belong to.

Four Groups of Fears

Group 1: If you're afraid of crashing and you believe your fear actually discriminates between the planes that will crash and those that won't, you're in Group 1. You think of your fear the way the comic book character, Spider Man, thinks of his tingling "spidey sense," which alerts him whenever there is danger. If this is what you actually believe, you probably don't really want to overcome the fear. Why would anyone want to overcome a fear that accurately tells them which planes are dangerous and which aren't? That would be a useful skill, and if you had it, pilots everywhere would want to be your friend. But I find it very hard to believe that anyone actually possesses such a skill. If you believe you do, this book will probably not be much help to you (a true psychic wouldn't have had to read this far to know this!).

However, there's a difference between continuing to have fearful thoughts you suspect are unreliable and actually believing them to be true predictors. Sometimes people experience doubts about a flight (or many other topics) and struggle hard to feel 100 percent sure that nothing will go wrong, only to find that their doubts grow stronger as they try to disprove and silence them. If that's your situation, you probably belong in Group 3. Group 1 is only for people who are quite convinced that their fear can predict the future, at least with respect to flying.

Group 2: If you have a history of actual disruptive behavior on an airplane that got you in trouble with the crew or authorities, you're in Group 2. You should refrain from flying until you can find ways to alter the behavior that got you in trouble. Seek out a consultation with a psychologist or other mental health professional, but first review your history carefully. It's surprisingly common for people who have cried on an airplane, or shouted out when startled by turbulence, or grabbed the hand of the passenger next to them, or asked to be let off the airplane, to think that these were signs of being out of control. That's just you showing your fear and then feeling embarrassed about it. If you only did something you found embarrassing, or even annoying, that doesn't put you in this group. Group 2 is only for people who actually got in trouble with authorities because they broke the rules and acted in some out of control way. If you just feared doing it, or showed your fear and felt embarrassed without actually getting into trouble, this is not your group.

Group 3: If you're afraid of crashing and can see, at least most of the time, that your fear doesn't discriminate between safe flights and dangerous flights, then you're in Group 3. Your fear doesn't offer a useful, valid signal about your flight. It just keeps repeating the same thing: "This plane is unsafe!" That's what tells you that it's a false alarm. Your fear doesn't offer you any useful information about how you can live a safer, longer life. It's like being stuck at a party with someone who talks too much. You might have to listen for a while, and that's annoying, but you don't have to take the content of their conversation seriously, and sooner or later, you'll be able to leave.

Group 4: If you're afraid of losing control of yourself as a result of your fear, and you have this fear whenever you fly or attempt to fly but have never done anything out of control on a flight, then your fear doesn't discriminate, either. It always says the same thing: "You're going to lose control of yourself and have a calamity!" Maybe you're afraid you'll start screaming, charge the cockpit, or try to kick open a window. Maybe you're afraid you'll be "scared to death" and have a heart attack, or "lose your mind" to fear. Maybe you keep having the thought, "What stops me from doing something crazy?" If you persistently have these and similar thoughts while you sit there like any other passenger, doing nothing disturbing, this is your group. You've become conditioned to feel afraid in the passenger situation, but it doesn't accurately predict any actual trouble for you.

---

1. Is your main fear crashing? If yes, go to question #3.

2. Is your main fear losing control of yourself while "trapped" on the plane? If yes, go to question #4.

3. If your fear is crashing, do you firmly believe your fear can accurately predict which planes will crash and which will arrive safely? If yes, you belong in group 1. If no, you belong in group 3.

4. If your fear is losing control, have you ever acted out of control on an airplane and been arrested or otherwise detained by the crew or authorities? If yes, you belong in group 2. If no, you belong in group 4.

Take a few minutes now to review these groups and decide which one fits your situation.

If you placed yourself in Group 1, you have beliefs that will probably prevent you from using the methods in this book, and if you want to fly, you will probably first need to get professional help to examine those beliefs. If you placed yourself in Group 2, you have a history of behavior that might make you unsuitable as a passenger, and if you want to fly, you may first need to get professional help to change that pattern or behavior.

If you can see that you belong in Groups 3 or 4, the path is clear for you to use this book to learn how to handle a false alarm and regain your ability to be a passenger on commercial flights.

CHAPTER 3

The Nature of Your Fear

· ·

Tom (not his real name) had a typical case of aviophobia. He had flown frequently as a child, a teenager, and a young adult during his early twenties. He never had any trouble with flying and traveled quite a bit, including several trips abroad. When he started working as a financial analyst after college, he often had to travel for work, and did so routinely without difficulty.

Tom's early work years were quite successful, and he advanced rapidly. However, there came a time when his career path slowed down, when the financial industry suffered a decline, and he began worrying more about retaining his existing job than thinking of what future position he might seek. At about the same time, he and his wife were blessed with two babies in three years.

It was in this context that Tom's relationship with flying began to change. Tom used to make good use of his time on board airplanes, either resting or getting some work done. He found himself increasingly unable to do either and felt much more restless than before. He resented the necessity of spending hours on board an airplane, out of contact with his family and his staff. He began to notice, with irritation and dislike, the minor bumps and noises he routinely used to overlook when he didn't mind flying. He began to feel confined on board the airplane, whereas before he used to enjoy the luxury of not having to take any phone calls or other interruptions. Now the flights seemed an unwanted intrusion.

Tom's first real difficulty with fear came when his plane was waiting to take off, and he felt restless, warm, and had trouble catching his breath. Just as he was about to summon the flight attendant, the captain announced that they would take off momentarily. Tom "made it" through the flight, but felt apprehensive the entire time, worrying about the physical sensations he was experiencing. He finished his trip and made the return flight home without incident, but the next time he had a scheduled flight, he only got as far as the airport. While waiting in the gate he started sweating, noticed his heart racing, and felt unable to breathe. He left the airport, later saw his physician, and was advised that he'd had a panic attack. Tom struggled for several years with this fear, "white knuckling" his way through some flights and canceling others at the last minute and driving instead, until the fear became so persistent that he stopped flying entirely. It was then that he sought help for the fear.

Tom's case had a happy ending because he was able to overcome his fear and resume flying whenever it suited him. He did so by using the methods I describe in this book. His story is representative of many people who fear flying. If, like Tom, you've become afraid of flying, you probably still want to fly because you recognize, at least in advance, how disproportionate your fear is. But your fearful thoughts become more frequent and persistent as the day of a flight approaches. As your fears grow, you're likely to try, harder and harder, to calm down and stop feeling afraid. These efforts to literally talk yourself out of the fear will fail, for reasons I'll cover shortly. When your efforts to get rid of your fear fail, you might end up treating your fear more seriously, as if it were a genuine threat, rather than the disproportionate worry it is. At that point, you'll be sorely tempted to end the fear by canceling your trip.

Canceling the trip will feel good, for a few moments, as soon as you do it. But you're likely to feel unhappy about it afterward. Moreover, canceling trips out of fear usually strengthens your phobia, making future trips more difficult. It's a bad trade in which you give up large amounts of future freedom for a few moments of temporary comfort.

The history of a fearful flier usually includes most, if not all, of the steps that Tom experienced.

- A history of flying without difficulty

- A change in life circumstances, including good changes, which might make life feel more challenging

- Unexpected anxiety during a flight

- An effort to not feel anxious

- The antianxiety effort fails, and the anxious feeling continues

- A vicious cycle of feeling afraid, trying to dispel it, failing to do so, and feeling worse as a result

- The fear becomes a phobia. Flying is frequently avoided, or endured with great difficulty

Two Key Assumptions About Fear

There are two common assumptions people make that give this fearful pattern its power.

1. If I'm afraid, then I'm in danger.

If this were always true, the anxiety and panic you feel before a flight would be a bad sign indeed. However, it's quite common and ordinary to feel fear in situations that are ordinarily safe; it's even common to feel afraid when you know quite well that you are safe.

To see how you can feel afraid even if you know there is no danger, look no further than scary books and movies. Millions of people around the globe regularly read and watch them and feel afraid, despite knowing that the stories are fiction and the events they depict are not actually occurring. There are a number of interesting points about the scary amusement industry, but to me, the most interesting fact is that *it works*. Humans are able to feel fear after simply looking at scary pictures or reading words. If we didn't have that capacity, Stephen King would be writing for *Good Housekeeping*!

To feel afraid, we only need the expectation, or anticipation, of danger, even if it only comes from a fictional movie or story. Or from a phobia. A phobia is very much like your own private scary movie in your mind.

So fear doesn't always signal danger. It's easy and common to become afraid even when you know you're not in danger.

2. I should be able to talk myself out of this fear.

Here's a sentiment I have heard from fearful fliers, time and again: "I know better, but it doesn't help!" Have you ever struggled with that thought?

It's frustrating. You can recognize the fears are exaggerated and disproportionate. But knowing this doesn't help you become unafraid. In fact, fearful fliers often tell me that the harder they try to feel calm, the worse the fear gets.

The fact that most fearful fliers used to fly without fear lends strength to this belief, because it doesn't make sense to most people that they're now afraid of something they used to do so easily. They naturally want to get back to their pre-fear status, and so they struggle against the fear, trying to "get back" to their former self, with counterproductive results.

How Your Brain Works

This problem usually arises because you have some unfair and unrealistic expectations of yourself and your brain. Let me explain.

Most of us, when we think about our brains, think of the part that creates conscious thought. It's called the cerebral cortex. When you're reminding yourself to pick up milk, memorizing facts for an exam, or fuming about an insulting comment you heard recently, that's your cerebral cortex at work. It's the part of the brain that allows you to think, and talk to yourself, and imagine what will happen in the future.

But it's only one of many parts of the brain, and most of those parts operate outside of our conscious awareness. One of those parts is largely responsible for strong emotional responses, and particularly for fight-or-flight responses. It's called the amygdala. If you're crossing the street and find yourself jumping back onto the sidewalk as a bus lurches your way, even before you consciously "knew" the bus was approaching, that's your amygdala at work.

It'll help for you to know a few things about how the amygdala works.

The Amygdala

Your amygdala gets pictures and sounds from the outside world before they reach any other part of your brain. It has fast, direct connections to your auditory and optic nerves, which bring information to the amygdala before it reaches the conscious, thinking part of your brain. That's because your amygdala is in charge of responding to threats, and that job has to be done as quickly as possible to ensure your survival.

Your amygdala learns by creating simple associations, like "dog" and "bad." It doesn't engage in complex thought like the cerebral cortex does, it just forms associations. These associations get stored in memory. You can think of these memories as little grooves etched into the brain surface, much like music that has been etched into records (prior to the advent of digital recordings!).

The nerves that connect the amygdala and your cerebral cortex are almost all one-way paths. The amygdala can send information to the cortex. The cortex can't send information directly back to the amygdala. This is why you can't talk yourself out of your fear. The amygdala isn't listening! It won't take your calls!

And it's a good thing the amygdala isn't listening, because it needs to operate as quickly as possible in the face of a possible emergency. Relative to the amygdala, the cerebral cortex is slow, much too slow for dealing with sudden emergencies. The amygdala doesn't have time to listen to the much slower operations of the cerebral cortex. Imagine the internal dialog of your cerebral cortex when it sees something resembling a wolf. It's like a committee of old guys. "Hey, was that a wolf or a dog?" "I remember one time, I saw an animal that looked like a half wolf, half bear. It was in Vietnam, 1971, and…" CHOMP! That's too slow for emergencies!

There are two kinds of errors we can make. Type 1 errors are called **false positives**, when we think that something is present when it's not. A soldier on sentry duty who thinks he sees enemies approaching the camp and fires his weapon when there are only rabbits out there has experienced a Type 1 error. No harm done, except maybe to the bunnies. Type 2 errors are called **false negatives**, when we think something is absent although it's actually present. A soldier who doesn't notice enemies when they're approaching is liable to get killed as the result of his Type 2 error.

Nobody's perfect, and we're all prone to error. Guess which kind of error the amygdala favors? You'd be right if you picked Type 1. Your amygdala is much more likely to perceive a threat when there isn't one than it is to fail to see a real threat. Your amygdala isn't built for accuracy. It's built for survival. And that, more than anything else, is why we're all prone to see problems that don't actually exist. It helps our survival. It's not so good for comfort, but it helps us avoid possible dangers.

My wife and I were recently driving through a large parking lot when three things happened. First, I slammed on the brakes without "knowing" why. (That was my amygdala at work). Second, my wife screamed "Stop!" (that was her cerebral cortex screaming). Third, I saw (via my cerebral cortex) two young girls running in front of my (now unmoving) car. My amygdala did a good job! No one was hurt. I was pretty revved up, though, and needed a few minutes to settle down, before I resumed driving.

Right about now, you might be thinking that you'd like to have a good talk with your amygdala to try and get it to relax a little about flying. You can't! Your cerebral cortex can't "talk" to your amygdala. You can't send it a command to calm down. But there is a way you can retrain your amygdala. First, one more amygdala fact.

The amygdala only creates new learning, new associations, when it's activated. Do you know what I mean by "activated"? I mean when you've become really afraid, when you're freaked out. That's the only time the amygdala creates new learning, because its main job is to protect you from external threats, and that's what it's concerned with.

Exposure Therapy

Each time you become really afraid, the amygdala is paying close attention, pencil poised, ready to take notes. A person with, say, a dog phobia will become very afraid at the approach of a dog as the amygdala urges her to run away. If she runs away and the "threat" ends, the amygdala will etch that groove called "dog-bad" a little deeper, strengthening the fear of dogs. However, if she hangs out with the dog even while feeling afraid and gives the fear a chance to peak and pass, the amygdala will then etch a new groove, "dog-okay." She still has the "dog-bad" groove in her brain, and that's still bigger and deeper than "dog-okay," so it will still be the dominant response to the appearance of a dog. But if she systematically practices spending time with dogs without fleeing, the amygdala will dig the "dog-okay" groove deeper and deeper, and it will, over time, become the new dominant response to the appearance of a dog.

This is the science behind exposure therapy. A dog phobic can use this method to lose her fear of dogs. And you can use it to lose your fear of flying. It's not about getting smarter, or tougher, or braver. It's about retraining your amygdala while respecting its role in the management of fight-or-flight responses.

Safety Behaviors

At this point, you might be wondering why Tom's fear didn't go away after he took a few more flights; it increased, instead. Weren't those flights he took after first becoming afraid examples of exposure?

They weren't the right kind of exposure. There are helpful and unhelpful ways of doing exposure, and it's important to know the difference. If you have a dog phobia and only do exposure to dogs from behind a 10-foot fence; or with a baseball bat in your hands, ready to club the dog; or with a motorcycle running, so you can hop on and escape at a moment's notice; you're not going to get any reduction of fear from those efforts. Your amygdala will notice the protective steps you took—the fence, bat, and motorcycle—and continue to regard dogs as dangerous animals for which you need these protections.

Those protective steps are examples of what psychologists call "safety behaviors" and "safety objects." Safety behaviors are the efforts people make to control and eliminate their fear. Keeping your eyes closed in an effort to not notice you're on an airplane is a common safety behavior, as is watching the faces of the flight attendants for any sign of concern. Safety objects are objects that people bring with them, or wear, in the hope that these objects will calm their fears—a "lucky shirt," for instance. These often have a superstitious aspect. While safety behaviors and objects often provide a few moments of immediate relief, they almost always backfire in the long run. Over time, people attribute their safety to the safety behaviors and objects and feel increasingly dependent on them. This adds to their sense of vulnerability rather than helping them feel more confident. (Hereafter, I'll use the term "safety behaviors" to include both behaviors and objects).

Tom used a variety of safety behaviors each time he flew, and came to believe that they actually saved him from becoming too fearful. As he felt more dependent on the safety behaviors, he engaged in them more frequently and intensely, much as an alcoholic will need more and more alcohol to "steady his nerves." This led him to become less confident in himself, rather than more. It was this erosion of his confidence that led him to stop flying altogether.

From Fear to Phobia

People who fear flying almost always employ safety behaviors, and so you probably do as well. Take a few moments now and consider this. What are some of yours? Write down 2 or 3 of them now, and we'll return to this topic in Chapter 6.

_____

_____

Relying on safety behaviors is one of the factors that turns a fear into a phobia. A fear becomes a persistent phobia when you resist the fear and struggle to get rid of it. People literally become afraid of feeling fear. This leads them to struggle to prevent, avoid, and stop the feelings (and thoughts and sensations) of fear. The more they struggle, the more persistently afraid they feel. Safety behaviors are one of the primary tools they use in this struggle.

So here is a central, and for many people, quite surprising, point about the fear of flying: What you really need to overcome is not the fear itself, but the habits of avoiding and struggling against the fear. It's typically the efforts people make to stop feeling afraid that actually sustain and strengthen their phobia.

Let's go back to scary movies for a moment. If you look closely at how people respond to scary movies, you'll see some responses that are probably similar to how you may respond to being afraid on a flight.

Some people will flee the theater, just as some fearful fliers will refuse to board the plane or will exit before takeoff. This will probably make the fear more persistent and future flights more difficult to board.

But let's think about the people who stay. Lots of people who might otherwise flee the theater feel obliged to stay, perhaps because they drove their friend to the theater and don't want to make him leave early or walk home, or perhaps because their friend has the car. These moviegoers often have the same thought fearful fliers do, of being "trapped" in the theater. They occupy themselves with various safety behaviors in an effort to "get through" the movie.

For instance, they might close their eyes in an effort to take in less of the scary story. They might try to distract themselves from the movie by playing with their cell phone, or tying their shoes, or getting very involved with their popcorn. They might tell themselves "it's only a movie!" They might reach over and grab on to the person next to them. That's probably okay to do, if they came in with that person!

Lots of fearful fliers employ the same kinds of methods. But notice that none of these methods actually reduce the fear of a movie. They help the moviegoer "get through" the movie and stay long enough to drive the friend home, but these methods are still keeping the moviegoer on edge, constantly struggling to keep the fear at bay. If they had to come back and see the same movie in a few weeks, they would probably feel more reluctant to enter the theater, because they would expect to feel afraid again.

Being afraid of a scary movie is no big deal. If you don't like the movie, or scary movies in general, there's no difficulty in avoiding them. You probably wouldn't have to go back to see the movie again. But having to avoid the fastest and safest mode of travel we have is a big problem for a lot of people. We'll get back to that in a moment.

What would you do if you wanted to truly lose your fear of a movie that had really scared you? I don't mean to just get through it. I mean, what if you wanted to get to a point where the movie no longer scared you, and maybe even seemed boring? (I doubt anyone cares enough about movies to do this, but this will be a helpful example, so bear with me).

What do you think? What would your strategy be for losing your fear of a movie that scared you a lot?

_____

_____

You get bonus points if your answer was to watch that movie again and again until it became boring. This would mean not skipping over the scary parts or using any of the safety behaviors I mentioned earlier. This would mean watching the entire movie, over and over, all the way through. Do you have any doubt that if you watched it sufficiently, it would start to lose its power to disturb you? Even people who love scary movies so much that they have a favorite one find that, after they've watched it a few times, it starts to lose its appeal as it becomes familiar. It literally loses its scariness with repetition, so long as you're not actually resisting the fear!

This is exactly how exposure treatment works, and you can use exposure practice to overcome your fear of flying. You will learn how to fly *without* the safety behaviors, rather than rely on them.

So what does it take to have a flying phobia? Two things. First, you have to develop a fear of flying, in ways I'll describe in the next chapter. Second, you have to actively oppose your fear. You have to resist your fear and have the mistaken belief that only by ridding yourself of your fear can you hope to fly again.

This is how people get fooled by the fear of flying. They think "First, I need to lose my fear, while I'm still on the ground, and then I can fly again." Trying to lose your fear while you're still on the ground just takes you into your head, where you argue with, and resist, your fears. People do this hoping and assuming it will help. Instead, it makes things worse. What you resist, persists.

You can lose your fear, but that will be the last thing that happens, rather than the first. How can you get there? You will need to fly again with your fears, because it's on the airplane that you can retrain your amygdala and learn to let go of your fears.

Now, let's take a look at how people become afraid of flying to begin with.

CHAPTER 4

How You Became Afraid of Flying

. . . .

As I noted in the previous chapter, many fearful fliers flew for years without difficulty before becoming afraid, and this frustrates them. They think repeatedly that they didn't always have this problem, and so they shouldn't have it now! But this thought just leads you to feel more resentful and resistant, making a solution more difficult.

So, it will probably be helpful to get a better understanding of how people develop this fear. To begin with, some people are more likely than others to develop a phobia or some other type of anxiety disorder. Some people are good candidates, and some are not.

Are You a Good Candidate for Aviophobia?

Several factors contribute to the likelihood of developing a fear of flying. One is genetic predisposition. Anxiety disorders are more frequent in some families than others, and this is usually due to various forms of genetic predisposition. Some people are simply born to be better candidates for this kind of trouble. Most people have personal challenges in life, and if you're afraid of flying, this is one of yours.

Attitude toward control is another factor. Fearful fliers are often people who particularly like to control events around them, and they would also like to control the thoughts and feelings they experience. They don't like to sit idle, the way you sometimes need to do in a waiting room, or an airplane, because they often feel restless there, and they struggle against that.

Are there others in your family history, maybe back a generation or more, who have similar phobias, or trouble with anxiety?	**Y**	**N**
Do you prefer driving a car to being a passenger?	**Y**	**N**
Do you get restless or annoyed while waiting for an appointment in a waiting room?	**Y**	**N**
If you're making plans to have lunch with a friend, would you rather be the one to select the restaurant?	**Y**	**N**
Do you often have thoughts you don't want and make an effort to stop thinking them?	**Y**	**N**

And, while all phobias are learned fears to some degree, some fears are easier to learn than others. We're naturally prepared to be afraid of certain objects and activities that were dangerous in a more primitive environment. These fears had survival value at earlier times in our evolutionary history. It's relatively easy to become afraid of heights, closed spaces, and certain animals like snakes. It's more difficult to develop fears of objects and situations that were never threatening to humans, like rabbits or trees.

So, some people are more likely than others, or "better candidates," to develop phobias. And some phobias are easier to learn than others. But if you are a "candidate" for this, you probably still need to go through certain experiences in order to become afraid of flying. There are some common patterns.

How Do People Develop Aviophobia?

Some people develop the fear in response to an unpleasant or scary flight. For instance, Steve, who attended one of my flying workshops, was a daredevil in his early twenties. He flew in the military, rode motorcycles cross country (without a helmet!), and camped in bear territory, all without fear. But that didn't stop him from suddenly developing a terrible fear of flying when a cross-country flight ran into some turbulence. The turbulence was fairly mild; some passengers slept through it, and others continued reading, watching movies, and doing crossword puzzles. Turbulence is only dangerous if you're not buckled in. But Steve became terribly afraid and wondered why the pilot wasn't telling them what was happening. He imagined himself rushing the cockpit, banging on the door, and demanding that the plane take him back home. He held tightly onto his seat, hoping to control himself this way. His mind raced, he sweat profusely, and he dearly wished he had never gotten on that plane. He told God that, if he should get home safely, he'd never fly again. And he didn't, for more than 10 years, until he realized how much freedom he had lost and decided to find a way to get it back.

Some people experience growing anticipation and anxiety about flying, even though they have flown without trouble for years, in response to changes in their life. Susan, a new mother of twins, experienced this pattern. She, too, had flown for years without trouble, but since the birth of her daughters, found herself increasingly anxious on flights and increasingly reluctant to schedule another. This was a particular problem for Susan because she had business trips most months of the year. She never had a notably "bad flight," as Steve did, but found herself dreading each flight a little more than the previous one. She was afraid that the plane would crash and she would die, leaving her babies without a mother. She also feared that she would become so afraid as to "lose her mind," and that her babies would thereafter have a crazy mother. One day she burst into tears when the cab arrived to take her to the airport, and she canceled her trip. She was unable to board another airplane for several years before seeking help.

Sometimes a preexisting phobia or anxiety problem gets connected with flying. For instance, a person with a fear of elevators and other tight spaces might find that the fear spreads to airplanes. A person who has been experiencing panic attacks in crowded situations that are difficult to leave quickly, such as churches and movie theaters, might find that this panic spreads to flying.

Some people experience a first panic attack as part of a broader panic disorder while on a flight. Sam, an attorney who flew frequently for business, experienced this one day while waiting for his flight to take off. He had been thinking how much he resented all the travel his job required when the door clanged shut and the plane backed away from the gate. He felt light-headed; his heart raced; his chest ached. He felt trapped and feared he was having a heart attack. His physician said he'd had a panic attack, but Sam found this hard to believe. He felt sure that all those physical symptoms could only be caused by a powerful physical disease. Sam's fear of having another episode led him to avoid flying for more than two years and caused him a lot of trouble with his employer.

Some people develop aviophobia in reaction to stories they hear or read. Larry, a bank executive, flew frequently without any difficulty until his early thirties, when he saw some graphic footage of a plane crash on television. He became preoccupied with wondering how such a thing could happen, and began searching for information about airline safety and plane crashes on the Internet. He found plenty of statistics that showed crashes to be extremely rare, but got caught up in an obsessive effort to prove that he would never be involved in a crash. It's impossible, of course, to prove that some event, however unlikely, will never occur in the future, and his desire for a guarantee led him to do more and more searching for perfect reassurance. The more he searched, the more anxious he became and this led him to start skipping flights.

About Turbulence

Turbulence is a shift in air currents from multiple causes: thunderstorms, jet streams, passing over different terrain like mountain ranges and deserts, warm or cold fronts, microbursts, and changes in atmospheric pressure. While people frequently refer to "air pockets" to describe the experience of the plane moving in response to turbulence, there is no such thing as an "air pocket" because there is no place in the atmosphere that's not filled with air. Turbulence is more accurately described as the airplane riding waves that travel through the air, just as a boat rides waves that travel through the water, and it rises and descends with the wave beneath it. Ships don't encounter "water pockets" and airplanes don't encounter "air pockets."

Pilots typically have no concern about turbulence damaging airplanes, because they've been built to withstand far more pressure. One pilot explained it to me this way: "If I'm flying freight, I just go right through it. But I try to dodge it when I have passengers, because I know it makes them uncomfortable." From his perspective, the only potential danger from turbulence is to passengers and crew who aren't safely buckled in.

Partly because plane crashes are so rare, the coverage of crashes, and especially the coverage of what are dubbed "near misses," is way out of proportion to the coverage of other life-threatening events. This makes crashes seem more frequent than they actually are.

Stories of passengers who run amok on an airplane and get tied up and turned over to the authorities similarly attract more than their share of media coverage. I always feel bad when I see one of these stories, because I know that millions of people with aviophobia or panic disorder are going to think this means it will happen to them. The truth is, the people who get into these altercations aren't people with panic disorder or phobias. Alcohol or drugs are usually involved, and this is why the people are acting "out of control." Sometimes the explanation is a mental health problem far more severe than panic disorder, like paranoia or psychosis.

Sometimes people experience a first panic attack on a plane in response to something they've done—maybe a weekend of partying too hard, with too much alcohol or other substances; maybe a gambling or other recreational weekend with too little sleep; or some other way of stretching themselves too thin. These people sometimes get stuck on blaming themselves because they link this behavior with the panic. There might be a link, but it's also true that many, many people party too hard or stretch themselves too thin without developing a fear of flying. The ones who don't probably just aren't good candidates to develop this fear. So there's probably more than one factor that has to be present to develop this fear. If you've been blaming yourself for the contribution these behaviors made to the origin of your fear, maybe you can just learn the lesson it has to offer, forgive yourself, and move on to accept and solve the problem. There's no reason to think that blaming yourself for this problem will be part of the solution.

People become afraid of flying in a variety of ways. Some are afraid of crashing; most are afraid of having a panic attack on the plane. In either case, they can struggle with the fear for years and years, continuing to fly, often relying on medications or alcohol, until it becomes such a struggle that one day they can't drag themselves on board a scheduled flight.

Others can fly for years without any problem, and then suddenly develop a phobia and abruptly stop flying. That phobia may develop in response to a turbulent flight, or a panic attack on an airplane, maybe while flying at a busy or stressful time in their lives, and the fear they experience gets connected in their mind with flying. Maybe they get frightened by news stories of a crash or a "near miss." Maybe they are new parents who become obsessed with thinking about the potential tragedy of their children losing a parent.

How did you become afraid of flying? Did your fear arise suddenly, in response to a specific event, or was it developing for years? What symptoms did you experience? What did you think those symptoms meant? _____

_____

_____

People become afraid of flying in many different ways, but there is one way that people *don't* become afraid. People don't become afraid of flying because they conduct a research project to identify the most dangerous everyday activities they experience in life, discover that flying is one of the most dangerous things they do, and decide to give it up. No, that's not how people become afraid of flying! In fact, most fearful fliers recognize that their feared outcomes are unlikely and exaggerated, and realize that they routinely engage in daily activities that are far more dangerous than flying. At least they can recognize this until it's time to board, when their "what if?" thoughts run away with them.

Three-Step Process of Developing Fear

Developing the fear of flying is actually a three-step process, even though it can happen quite rapidly.

First, you get afraid, in one of the ways I just described, either on board an airplane or while anticipating a flight.

Then, you struggle against the fear, hoping to rid yourself of it before you fly again.

When you realize that your efforts to get rid of the fear aren't doing the job, your fear increases, and you struggle harder. You double down on the methods and responses that actually maintain and strengthen your fear. It's in this way that people get tricked into "putting out fires with gasoline." Ultimately, you may begin to avoid flying entirely.

Justifying the Fears

People often create explanations and justifications for their fear. Why do they do this?

We all like to have logical explanations for our life experiences. We like to think of ourselves as rational and want to be able to explain our experiences in rational terms. It seems irrational to become afraid of something that isn't particularly dangerous. So we all have a natural inclination, when we become quite afraid, to treat it as a sign of danger. Most people would rather think they're in danger than think that they're being irrational!

These are the explanations people usually develop:

- They blame the fear on flying. They tell themselves that it's not safe enough and persuade themselves that nobody should fly. The problem with this is that all the evidence indicates that flying is the safest form of travel and one of the safest forms of all human activity.

- They blame it on themselves. They tell themselves that they're too weak, too dumb, too cowardly, or too defective in some way, and so they feel embarrassed and ashamed of the fear. The problem is, these are usually very competent people who are not weak, dumb, cowardly, or defective.

- They blame it on the confinement they experience in the airplane, thinking that they can't tolerate staying in that crowded airplane with hundreds of others for hours without the ability to leave. The problem is, they've often sat in a chair that's no bigger than their airline seat for hours—at home, in a football stadium, at a concert, or at a funeral service—without any trouble. This has more to do with their thoughts about being "trapped" than it does the actual space and circumstances.

Which of these do you do? What do you tend to blame?

_____

_____

None of these explanations really describe the situation accurately, so they don't lend themselves to a solution. These theories instead lead you to get more stuck.

It's going to be a lot easier getting over this fear if you have a good understanding of what the problem is, one that leads you to solutions rather than blame and frustration.

Let's Talk About Safety (Just a Little)

You might be wondering, "Where is the chapter on safety statistics?"

What you see here is the entire section on safety statistics.

As this book is being written in 2017, approximately 24,000 flights take off and land every day in the continental United States. In 2016, there were a total of 719 million passengers on those domestic flights within the US. More than 2.2 million people flew on domestic flights across the US every single day. That's like having almost the entire population of Chicago up in the air, every day of the year. By way of comparison, there are only four cities in the United States that have more than 2 million inhabitants.

The risk of dying on any US domestic flight has been calculated to be less than 1 in 7 million. This means you would need to fly every day, for about 20,000 years, in order to be sure to die. (I guess you'd also want to live real close to the airport.)

This should mean there are hardly any deaths due to crashes. And that's exactly the case. If you look at the number of deaths in airline crashes between 2007 and 2012, there were zero deaths, none, in five of the six years. In 2009 there were 49 deaths. And in the seven years from 2010 to 2016, the number of deaths in American flights operating *anywhere in the world was*…zero. None in seven years.

If you're in Group 3, with a fear of crashing, you might have had some automatic thoughts or comments as you read these safety statistics. Did you notice them? Write them down here.

_____

_____

_____

_____

> Does this mean that there is no danger associated with flying? No, we can't truthfully say that. We can't say that because there's danger associated with every human activity. What we can say is that, compared to almost any other activity you might engage in, you are at less risk of death while flying on a commercial aircraft in the United States than you would be doing almost anything else, anywhere else. It's one of the safest places you can be! The fear of flying is radically disproportional to the risk involved. But every moment of life carries risk. After all, the cumulative mortality rate in the United States is shockingly high—100%!

In the United States, annual deaths due to auto accidents have totaled nearly 40,000 per year in recent years. This is why, if you ask pilots, "What's the most dangerous part of flying?" they'll usually say, "The drive to the airport." It's hard to find any form of human activity—riding a train, crossing the street, taking a prescription medicine, eating a steak, or sleeping in your cozy bed—that's actually safer than flying.

But most of you, even those in Group 3 who fear crashing, probably already know this, at least in general. And you've probably had well-intentioned people tell you of these facts, hoping it would somehow help you to lose your fear. And you've probably replied with, or at least thought of, a variety of replies.

- At least in a car, I can steer away from the trouble.

- At least in a train, I can hop off.

- At least if I'm on the ground, I can get to a hospital.

And so on. Were these some of the automatic thoughts you had? Still, an awful lot of people die in those cars they can steer, and hardly anybody ever dies in an airplane.

With fear of flying, that's not the point. It's all about the fear, not the flying. You need to get better at handling fear, not flying. Because this is a fear of fear.

People have written entire books about how and why commercial flying is safe, but I'm not going to spend any more time on the topic. Fearful fliers I've worked with usually came to see me already knowing a lot about safety and safety statistics. Unfortunately, it didn't help them much. It frustrated them, and they would say things like, "I know it's safe, but that doesn't help!"

The reason it didn't help was they were hoping to remove their fear while they were still on the ground and figured they would fly once that job was done. That doesn't work for most people. It just maintains and strengthens the fear.

If you want to learn more about airline safety and how flying "works," that would be okay. But be aware that many people who fear flying get caught up in an obsessive search for information that will prove to them, beyond the shadow of a doubt, that nothing can ever go wrong and that they are guaranteed to be safe. No one can get such a guarantee—not about flying, or anything else.

Flying with Your Fears

It frequently happens, when the time for our workshop flight draws near, that one of the participants will ask me to guarantee that nothing will go wrong. This is the problem that Larry experienced, seeking a perfect guarantee that truly isn't available, and becoming more anxious as a result. I have to tell them I can't do that, because I don't know the future any more than anyone else. And I know, if I were foolish enough to offer this guarantee anyway, the very next question they would ask is, "How can you be so sure?" What I do tell them, what I do guarantee, is that I will be getting on the plane.

Don't try too hard to be sure, or to remove all your fears, especially while you are on the ground. The goal of "being sure" that nothing bad will ever happen is a mirage. No matter how fast you drive toward a mirage down the road, you'll never get there. It continually recedes into the distance. And so long as you struggle in an effort to oppose and rid yourself of the fear, the goal of being fearless will elude you. This isn't a problem you can think your way through, or argue away, or bring to an end by will power. Once having acquired the fear of flying, the most effective way out is to respond in a counterintuitive way, to practice with the fear rather than against it. You won't lose your fear while you're just thinking about flying, on the ground. You'll learn to let go of the fear on board an airplane.

Here are some key points in the process of arranging a flight. At each point, you can easily get ambushed by "what if" thoughts suggesting whatever calamity you fear. If you are in Group 3, it would be a thought about crashing, and if you're in Group 4, some loss of control. It might seem to you as though you need to do something about that thought—to dispute or argue with it, to distract yourself, to protect yourself against the "threat" it describes, to get reassurance from others, or to medicate it away. That would be an intuitive response, a "common sense" response, but that would probably increase, rather than reduce, your anxiety.

For each of these steps below, identify a counterintuitive response you could use. The first one has been done for you as an example.

STEP	INTUITIVE RESPONSE	COUNTERINTUITIVE RESPONSE
Considering a practice flight	Plan to think about it some other time	Look at airline website to identify a one-hour trip
Reserving a flight	Get flight info, but postpone purchase	

STEP	INTUITIVE RESPONSE	COUNTERINTUITIVE RESPONSE
Pack luggage	Postpone packing to avoid worry or pack more safety objects	
Go to the airport	Call friend for reassurance or distraction while in transit	
Board the plane	Wait until the plane is ready to depart	
Waiting on board for departure	Exit plane when you feel panicked	

When you've completed this book, come back to this exercise and review your answers, because you'll be in a much better position to resolve these concerns once you've finished the book.

Of course, it's true that a person who fears flying will get some immediate relief by canceling a flight. People who go so far as to get to the airport but then turn around and leave feel better as soon as they start heading for the exits. Unfortunately, that increased comfort doesn't last. By the time they get to the parking lot, they're already feeling regret that they didn't see it through. And their desire or need to fly still remains.

It will go better for you if you allow yourself to have these fearful thoughts, rather than oppose them. Don't waste time and energy looking for more evidence of what you already know, hoping to eradicate your fear. You'll be better able to let go of your fear once you get some more experience flying with your fears.

Two Main Points on Fear

So, there are two main points I want you to notice from this chapter. The first is that this fear is your problem, but it's not your fault. You did not become afraid of flying because of some mistaken action or thought. Rather, it's the result of numerous environmental and biological influences. It's too bad you have it. It is a problem, which you either need to solve or leave unsolved. But don't get fooled into thinking this is your fault and blaming yourself. Blame is not part of the solution. Everybody's got some problems, and this is one of yours.

The second point is that people are naturally inclined to take their thoughts literally, and either argue with them, trying to prove to themselves that their fears are mistaken, or agree with the thoughts and try to justify them. Both reactions are understandable, but both tend to make your situation more difficult rather than better.

You'll be better off treating these worrisome thoughts just like other symptoms of fear. All they mean is "I'm nervous." Don't try to suppress them, argue with them, or justify them. They're just symptoms of nervousness, and the best response is to allow yourself to feel nervous and work with it, rather than against.

Is it okay to accept feeling nervous? Yes, because this fear is a false alarm, rather than a signal fear. It's an instance of becoming afraid in the absence of any unusual danger. You don't need to make yourself safer. You're probably already as safe as you can be.

Is it beneficial to accept feeling nervous? Yes, because when you resist the fear, you're likely to get "tricked" into making it worse rather than better.

We'll see how this trick works in the next chapter.

CHAPTER 5

The Panic Trick

....

If you're in Group 3 or 4, you can recognize, at least when you're not boarding a plane, that you have a false alarm that doesn't accurately predict any danger. Yet, still, the fear persists. Your fear doesn't point to a problem that you have to solve or protect against. Your fear *is* the problem. It's a fear of fear.

You've probably tried many ways to get rid of the fear. That's reasonable. If people could get rid of their fear by opposing it, no one would need to suffer with a phobia. If you had effective methods for resisting and stopping the fear, you probably wouldn't be reading this book. Maybe you'd be on a flight to Paris, successfully keeping your anxiety in check! Certainly, anyone who's ever been afraid of flying has tried, long and hard, to stop feeling afraid.

The problem is, those efforts to oppose anxiety tend not to work. Why is that?

ACT (acceptance and commitment therapy) therapists and proponents explain it this way: We deal with two main components in our lives. There's an external world of people and objects, and an internal world of thoughts, emotions, and physical sensations. These two worlds are very different and require very different handling.

Rule of thumb in the external world: The harder I try, and the more I struggle, the more likely I am to get what I want. It's not guaranteed, but I can increase my chances of getting what

I want out there by effort and struggle. And if I want to get rid of something in my external world, I can often do that. If I see someone has tossed a soda bottle on my lawn, I can pick it up and put it in the recycling bin, and it won't be back. I can get rid of it.

Rule of thumb in the internal world: The more I oppose something, the more I have of it. This is frequently demonstrated with the challenge "don't think of a white bear." This is an example of a paradox in which your effort to not think of something produces thoughts of the very topic you wanted to forget or dismiss.

If you have a song stuck in your head, the more you try to stop hearing the song, the more persistent it will become. If you have a scary thought about an upcoming event, the more you try to stop thinking about it, the more you're going to have that thought. And "getting rid of" something in the internal world is particularly difficult. While you can throw the soda bottle away for good, when you attempt to get rid of thoughts or feelings, they generally become more persistent.

Thought Stopping

A classic example of this is "thought stopping." This technique used to be recommended rather widely, and is unfortunately still with us, although in my view, it has no merit whatsoever. It involves snapping a rubber band against your wrist when you have the unwanted thoughts while thinking (or saying) "STOP!"

This doesn't work; in fact, it makes the thought more persistent and frequent, and so it actually makes you feel worse. Nothing could be less helpful than thought stopping! In fact, don't even think about thought stopping!

The fear of flying is all about the thoughts, emotions, and physical sensations you experience when boarding a plane, or even when you're just thinking about flying. It's all about uncomfortable stuff in your internal world. Our typical gut instinct, when we feel something unpleasant, is to get rid of it. It's to treat it the way we treat that soda bottle on the lawn. But while we can throw the bottle away and ensure that it never comes back, when we try to toss out our thoughts, emotions, and physical sensations, it's like tossing boomerangs. They keep coming back.

In your internal world of thoughts, emotions, and physical sensations, *what you resist persists*. When you struggle against your fear and try not to be afraid, your resistance will maintain and strengthen the fear, rather than reduce it.

No wonder so many people try so hard with such poor results!

Have you ever had a friend or relative who, hoping to help you overcome this problem, suggested you simply "get over it"? Or who, upon hearing you voice your fears about a flight, urged you to "stop thinking about it"? Or, hoping to challenge and remove your fear, demanded to know, "Why are you so afraid? It's silly!"

How did those "helpful hints" work out for you? If you're like most fearful fliers, or people with any kind of phobia, they weren't helpful at all. You probably know that from experience. And you know what else? They're not any more helpful when you do them to yourself.

When people don't accept, for the present, their fear of flying, it leads them to more struggle. They blame themselves for not being able to simply stop being afraid. And they blame the flight industry for all kinds of sins, some real, and some imagined. Neither of these paths helps them feel better about flying. Rather, they feel worse, and more afraid.

I don't mean that you need to accept you will always have this problem. I simply mean that you'll be better off accepting the symptoms of fear rather than resisting them, and that this will help bring you to the point of letting go of the fear. For instance, fearful fliers often try so hard to stop thinking about the aspects of a flight that scare them, maybe the closing of the door, or the length of the flight. As they gather their belongings and prepare to go to the airport, they try hard to keep such thoughts at bay. Maybe they also ask family members not to mention their feared topics.

If this actually helped, it would probably be okay. All too often, though, this effort at limiting and censoring your thoughts backfires. It works like efforts to ban books. It keeps bringing your attention back to the banned material! Later in this book I'll suggest methods that can actually help, where you allow yourself to have the thoughts (thoughts that will probably come anyway), rather than trying to banish or distract from them.

Do you have thoughts about flying that you resist, or try to avoid? List three in the space provided on the next page.

I know that simply writing them down might make you feel nervous, but remember what you're doing here. You're learning how to defang these thoughts, how to have them without feeling so nervous. You can do that by practicing exposure, by getting used to them rather than protecting against them. So, if you're willing, allow yourself to feel anxious and write down three of the thoughts you try to avoid.

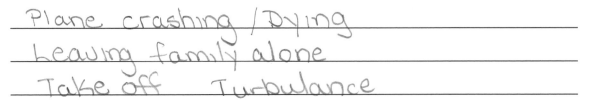

Plane crashing / Dying
Leaving family alone
Take off   Turbulance

If these thoughts were written in a foreign language, one you didn't know, then they wouldn't lead you to feel nervous. Would you agree that's true? If you don't know how to read German or Portuguese and they were written in either of those languages, they would have no effect on you.

Want to try something silly? Say these thoughts aloud in a bad German accent. All three of them. Or use a bad French accent, if you prefer.

What's that like? How does it affect the way you react to the scary thoughts?

It's interesting to try this. I bet most people who try this find that the use of a silly accent changes their emotional reaction. Even though they know what the words mean, the slight addition of an accent changes their reaction a bit, or maybe a lot.

And if the simple addition of a silly accent changes the way you feel about scary thoughts, then there's plenty of room to hope, maybe expect, that you can change how you feel about flying.

Understanding the Panic Trick

There's a Panic Trick that's central to all phobias: You experience discomfort and treat it like danger.

When I say "discomfort," I mean all the different ways in which you feel afraid: the scary thoughts, the physical sensations, the powerful emotions, and the fearful behaviors of avoidance and escape.

Fearful fliers I've worked with have sometimes pointed out that discomfort seems like a mild word for the fear they experience. I agree, but I wanted a word that begins with a D, and this was the best I could do. This comparison is the fork in the road, and I wanted to make it easier to remember: Is it Danger or Discomfort? If you remember this question when you become afraid and get a good handle on it right away, it will make it easier for you to respond to fears in a helpful way.

When I say "danger," I mean the dangers that you typically fear. For Group 3, it's crashing. For Group 4, it's misbehaving so badly and acting so out of control that the crew and passengers have no choice but to overpower you; freaking out and losing your mind; or having a stroke or heart attack, literally "dying of fright."

Let's break this down. The Panic Trick occurs when you experience discomfort and treat it like danger. What's good for danger? Evolution, over millions of years, has given us three ways of handling danger: fight, flight, and the less well-known freeze. If it looks weaker than me, I'll fight it; if it looks stronger and slower than me, I'll run away from it; and if it looks stronger and faster than me, I'll freeze like a possum and hope it doesn't see so well. That's all we have for danger: fight, flight, or freeze.

This response starts with a signal from your amygdala that activates the sympathetic nervous system, triggering your adrenal glands to pump adrenaline into your bloodstream. The adrenaline creates changes throughout your body that will give you an advantage in fighting off, or running away from, a predator. It increases your heart rate and blood pressure; redistributes blood away from your skin and digestive tract and toward your muscles, heart, and other vital organs; speeds up your breathing; opens your pupils wider to enhance vision; and releases blood sugar (a source of energy) into your bloodstream.

You might also experience two side effects to the rapid energizing of your body. First, these physical changes create heat, and your body temperature starts to rise. So you naturally do what we all do to cool ourselves—you sweat! And this sweating has an additional advantage. If you're struggling with a predator, it's good to be slippery!

Second, blood will flow away from your digestive tract toward your muscles and vital organs. This will bring a sudden stop to your digestion if you've eaten recently. No point wasting energy digesting your food when a predator is trying to make a meal out of you! The halt in digestion may create some stomach discomfort.

Your amygdala is just trying to keep you safe. But what you have here is a failure to communicate! This can occur when the amygdala of, say, a dog phobic notices a dog, or an elevator phobic notices an elevator, or a flying phobic notices an airplane, or even just thinks of one.

You and your amygdala are built for survival, not accuracy, and so are very likely to get tricked into responding to the initial discomfort of the phobic cue—the dog, elevator, or airplane—and treat it like danger rather than discomfort.

Your amygdala's just making sure! It's pumped you full of adrenaline and energy and got you all ready for fight or flight. But there's nothing you need to fight or flee. False alarm! It's just discomfort.

What's good for discomfort? Here we have lots of variations of "chill out and give it time to pass." We don't need to oppose discomfort because it's a temporary bad feeling, not something that will harm us. Claire Weekes, an Australian physician who was the first person to write about panic and anxiety in truly helpful ways, offered the metaphor of floating with your anxiety. People were sometimes unclear what she meant by "float." I think she meant the opposite of swim: Make no effort, simply allow the environment to support you.

Learning to float is often the first task in learning to swim. Learning to swim involves lots of complicated movements that have to be well-coordinated: the strokes and paddling you do with your hands and arms, the kicking you do with your legs and feet, and the turning of your head to coordinate with your breathing. There's a lot to learn about swimming.

What's there to learn about floating? A block of wood can float. It can't swim, but it can float. Why? Because floating asks you to do nothing but lie there. That's easy for a block of wood—it never does anything.

That's not so easy for humans. We're used to doing things. We have to train ourselves to act like a block of wood, just hanging out, doing nothing. A block of wood makes a great passenger, once you get it into its seat. For you, with your squirming, grabbing the armrest, thinking of escape plans, watching for signs of trouble, and worrying about the future, it's more challenging.

This is why people often get tricked by panic. You have to do less, rather than more, and your instinct is to do more.

What gives the Panic Trick so much power is this: What's good for danger is the *opposite* of what's good for discomfort. For danger, we have fight, flight, or freeze. For discomfort, we have wait and give it time to pass. If you get fooled into treating your fear as a reliable sign of danger, then you're getting tricked into responding in ways that make you feel more afraid rather than less, and you're then much more likely to flee the airport and go home. There are several reasons for this, but fundamentally it's because no amount of fight, flight, or freeze will bring the fear to an end when there is no actual danger that you can prevent. There's no threat to hit or run away from. All that resisting not only fails to produce the guarantee of safety that you hope for, but it maintains and strengthens the anxiety by getting you pumped up for a struggle that doesn't occur.

How has the Panic Trick influenced your fear of flying? We'll take a look in the next chapter.

CHAPTER 6

What Have You Tried?

· ·

A very successful businessman called me one day to inquire about my workshop for fear of flying. When I explained that the workshop included a practice flight, he said, "Doc, I flew more than 100,000 miles last year. I was more afraid the last mile than the first one. How is more flying going to help me?"

He had a good point. More flying *in the same way he was used to flying* wouldn't be of any help. We talked a little more, and it came out that his way of flying included numerous safety behaviors, including the following:

- only flying on airlines he had used before

- bringing his lucky shirt (it was frayed, so he didn't want to wear it, but he kept it in his carry-on bag)

- trying to sit in the same row and seat every time he flew

- avoiding nighttime flights

- gripping the armrest throughout the flight

- monitoring the Weather Channel for days before the flight

- spending extra time meditating and exercising in the days before a flight, as if preparing for a martial arts bout

- keeping track of how many minutes remained before landing

- keeping his eyes closed when he wasn't checking the time

- drinking alcoholic beverages before and during the flight

He used a variety of techniques in an attempt to fight off and remove the anxiety. And the more he opposed the anxiety, the worse he felt. Each time he completed a flight, he felt it had been a close call, an experience he was barely able to tolerate only because of his safety behaviors, and he was left with the fearful thought, "What if it's worse next time and I can't control it?" Flying that way, in a struggle to control the anxiety, does lead a person to feel more anxious, and 100,000 miles of flying that way led him to feel a lot more anxious.

This is what turns a fear into a phobia. A fear becomes a persistent phobia when you resist the fear and struggle to get rid of it. People literally become afraid of feeling fear, which leads them to struggle to prevent, avoid, and stop the feelings (and thoughts and sensations) of fear. And the more they struggle, the more persistently afraid they feel.

If you're like most fearful fliers, you've already tried lots of things in an effort to stop feeling afraid of flying. And, since you're reading this book, you're still looking for solutions.

What's more, you may have found that the harder you try, the worse it gets. If you're like most fearful fliers, this observation has a bitter edge to it. It might seem to suggest that there's something wrong with you because as much as you try to solve this problem, it only becomes more difficult and permanent. Or maybe it seems to indicate that there just isn't any solution to this problem, that all your efforts are bound to fail.

But if it's true that the harder you've tried, the worse things have gotten, I think this tells you something entirely different. I think this tells you that you've been trying methods that actually make the problem worse! It's probably the case that the fault lies with the methods you've chosen, rather than you. And if that's true, all that shame and blame you've experienced has been a colossal waste of time.

I've already noted that fear of flying is a counterintuitive problem, one for which our gut instincts of how to solve it are usually wrong. It's common for people to get tricked into responding to their anxiety in ways that make it worse rather than better.

So it'll be helpful for you to take a good look at what you usually do to help yourself with the fear. There's probably a lot of things you do in an effort to feel less afraid.

First, consider how you try to manage your anticipatory anxiety in the days and weeks before a scheduled flight.

How do you respond to anxious thoughts about flying? It's common for people to try to make themselves stop thinking of an unpleasant topic. Many people repeatedly ask for reassurance from loved ones and the Internet. Some exercise intensively, while others drink more alcohol than usual. Some will try to "undo" the anxious thought, perhaps with a religious gesture like making the sign of the cross, or by trying to replace it with a calming thought. How do you try to handle your anticipatory anxiety? Make a list and hold on to it for later.

Once you think you have a fairly thorough list of the efforts you make in the days and weeks prior to a flight, move on to consider your behavior on the day of the flight. What do you do to try to relieve or prevent anxiety…

Just before leaving for the airport? _take xanax   discard_

At the airport while waiting to board? _get a drink   discard_

During the boarding process? _Look at crew_

On board the plane before it takes off? _listen to music /breath_

During the cruising part of the flight? _try to sleep_

During the landing? _Glad its over_

Do you bring any particular objects on board the plane, objects that you hope will help to keep your anxiety level down? _____

Common Safety Behaviors

Most fearful fliers rely on a lot of safety behaviors. As you may recall, these are anti-anxiety efforts that seem intuitively like they may be helpful, but actually result in more, rather than less, anxiety overall. I asked you to make a short starter list of several of your safety behaviors in Chapter 3.

Review that starter list now, if you made one, and make a good, thorough list of your safety behaviors by answering the questions on the previous page. Remember your efforts on past flights, or past attempts to fly, and write down everything you tried. Then take a look at my lists below. These will probably jog your memory about other efforts you made, and you can add them to your lists.

What have you done? It might seem to you as though you haven't done very much, but my experience with fearful fliers is that they've usually tried lots of things.

Here are some of the steps people often try during the two weeks or so before a flight, when they're trying to calm the anticipatory anxiety they feel.

Common Behavioral Changes Aimed at Anticipatory Anxiety

- Extra efforts to be healthy, with increased attention to diet, exercise, and sleep, as if in training for an athletic event.

- Increased use of alcohol, antianxiety medications, street drugs, or supplements.

- An unusual amount of time and effort devoted to meditation, relaxation, and other calming techniques, as if on an emergency basis.

- Watching the weather channel for advance information about your flight path and destination.

- Trying to be a better person, one more pleasing to God. Being more consistent at picking up after your dog, acting more kindly to others. Increased praying and attendance at church.

- Tidying up loose ends. Reviewing your will and financial plans, paying bills that will soon be due.

- If you live alone, emptying your refrigerator, making sure someone has a key to your home and car in case you don't make it back home.

- Arranging for others to adopt your pet(s) and plants in case you don't survive.

- Very thorough attention and excessive time given to packing your luggage, perhaps as a distraction or a strong desire to feel in control.

- Being more compliant with superstitious rules, even though you don't entirely believe in them.

Thoughts and Worries

- Thought stopping, distraction, and other efforts to undo or reverse scary thoughts.

- Seeking reassurance about your fears on the Internet.

- Avoiding unpleasant topics or activities, and avoiding the news media.

- Looking for signs—from God, the universe, or wherever—that all will be well.

- Reviewing your ticket and seat assignment, wondering if you should change it.

- Having thoughts of getting a rental car for the return trip, or of canceling the entire trip.

Interactions with Others

- Telling loved ones how much you love them, in case you don't get another chance, or leaving "last" messages in case you don't return.

- Seeking opinions about the flight; seeking reassurance that you will be okay.

- Trying to defend and justify your fear to others, often with arguing as a result.

- Trying to hide your fear from others.

Prior to Leaving for the Airport

- Rechecking the weather; recalculating travel time to the airport; reviewing your pack list.

- Checking and rechecking appliances, windows, light switches, and locks to be sure you haven't forgotten anything.

- Looking around your home, at photos and other sentimental objects, as if it's the last time.

- Reviewing your decision to travel and wondering if you should cancel.

- Drinking alcohol, or taking antianxiety medication.

- Praying for God to protect you.

- Treating minor decisions, like what shirt to wear, as if they will be of importance

At the Airport

- Waiting till the last minute to board or trying to pick the best moment.

- Engaging in superstitious behaviors or rituals as you board (e.g., touching the skin of the airplane for good luck).

- Drinking alcohol or taking antianxiety medication.

- Looking to see if the crew appears trustworthy and happy.

- Reviewing your decision to travel and wondering if you should change your mind.

- Trying to undo or remove the "wrong" thoughts that may occur to you.

- Calling friends or family for reassurance and encouragement

On Board the Plane

- Trying to sit in a "good seat," whatever you think that is, such as by a window or aisle, in the front or back of plane, or in lucky row numbers.

- Trying to pretend you are not on an airplane.

- Trying to distract yourself with reading, movies, games, and other items.

- Grabbing the armrest.

- Deliberately watching out the window, or avoiding it.

- Watching the faces of crew members for signs of panic.

- Watching the passengers for signs of fear or alarm.

- Scrutinizing the passengers to identify possible terrorists.

- Asking for information that's not available or guaranteed (Will we be on time? Will there be any turbulence?).

- Traveling with an emotional support animal, or a support person.

- Trying to hide your fear.

- Following rigid rules about staying in your seat, use of bathroom, eating.

- Wearing lucky clothes or carrying lucky objects.

- Looking at pictures of loved ones.

Does my list remind you of additional efforts you've made? Go back to your first draft and make any changes or additions.

Those of you in Group 3, who fear crashing—do you really do anything that makes the flight safer? Many fearful fliers engage in superstitious behaviors, such as trying to have the right thoughts as they board, touching the skin of the airplane for luck, and bringing various good luck charms, hoping to help the plane be safe. I had one overweight client who tried to help balance the plane by sitting a certain distance from other heavy people. If people really had these kinds of powers to create safety, I sure wish they'd use them on the highway!

Airline safety is actually due to the actions of those who work in the field—the pilots and crews, the air traffic controllers, the Federal Aviation Administration, and others. You're a passenger, and it's not your job to make the airplane safe. Look at the steps you take to calm yourself on board the plane. How would it make you safer to drink a beer, or distract yourself, or pet your comfort animal? Even though you fear crashing, you're likely engaging in the same efforts to stop feeling afraid as the people in Group 4. So even though your fears are different, the path out for Groups 3 and 4 will be largely the same.

You've probably tried any number of things in an effort to stop feeling afraid. How have they worked out for you? Have any of the efforts you've made to reduce your fear actually done so? Take a look at each item on your list and see if you find any that have actually reduced your fear over time.

You might think that some of these have helped you "get through" a flight, the same way that people close their eyes or look away during a scary movie, but those steps don't reduce fear going forward. In fact, they usually maintain and strengthen the fear. Grabbing and holding an armrest, for instance, creates more physical tension and leads you to think that your safety depends on the strength of your bicep, when the seat belt is already holding you in place without any effort on your part.

In the same way, relying on an alcoholic beverage or antianxiety medication will perhaps give you some temporary comfort, but it also reinforces the idea that you need these substances to be able to fly. And, of course, the need grows each time you rely on it, so you are likely to feel the need to use it again. You feel protected from your fear, which is very different from losing your fear. Your fear is similarly reinforced when you travel with the company of an emotional support animal or a support person. Anything that seems to protect you from your fear actually maintains the fear going forward, rather than removing it over time.

Do you have any items on your lists that have actually helped you become less afraid so that you became more willing to fly again? Or have they just helped you "get through" that particular moment at the price of making you more afraid the next time?

If you decide an item on your list actually contributes to you becoming less afraid in the future, mark it "KEEP." Each item that you decide that simply helps you "get through" but maintains or even increases your fear going forward, mark it "DISCARD."

Go ahead and mark up your lists now. Don't get too concerned with being sure or right, because you can always revise your opinions afterward. This will give you a first draft of a list of the safety behaviors you want to leave behind when you travel.

The fear of flying is a very common and persistent fear. The reason it persists is not that people don't try to stop feeling afraid. Most fearful fliers try lots of safety behaviors in an effort to stop feeling afraid. They just don't get much benefit from these efforts.

My clients often describe their history by saying that despite their best efforts to overcome it, they kept being afraid of flying. But that's actually not true. The truth is they kept being afraid of flying *because of* their best efforts. Their efforts to stop feeling afraid tend to backfire and sustain, rather than reduce, the fears.

As we've discussed, people resort to a variety of safety behaviors in an attempt to control or eliminate fearful emotions, physical sensations, and thoughts. And that's very hard to do. It's not like with physical objects: If, while you're waiting to board an airplane, you take a candy wrapper or beverage cup and throw it in the trash, it's not coming back. You can control, and remove, most objects around you if you wish. But if, after you throw away that cup, you try to remove the feeling of fear, or try to silence a scary thought you keep having about the flight, you'll probably find that the feeling or thought just becomes more persistent. In your internal world of thoughts, emotions, and physical sensations, what you resist, persists.

This is the reason you may have already noticed that "the harder you try, the worse it gets." It's not because you're some kind of weakling or knucklehead who can't execute a simple strategy. It's because you're using a strategy—trying to eliminate fear and anxiety with the use of safety behaviors—that makes it worse in the long run.

So, let's move on to develop a different strategy, one that will allow you to fly and gradually allow the fear to diminish.

CHAPTER 7

Flying with Fear

· ·

To recap, the fear of flying is not what it may seem. It's not a signal fear that gives you a reliable indication of danger. It's a false alarm that just tells you to be afraid. And, not only do people become afraid in the absence of danger, they also get tricked into opposing and resisting the fear in ways that increase it, rather than calming themselves down. The harder they try to calm themselves, the more chronically anxious they become.

One of the biggest obstacles people face in overcoming this fear is the idea that they need to lose their fear *before* they can fly. This is the idea that turns fears into phobias. When they try so hard to stop feeling afraid, it only strengthens the phobia.

Has this idea been part of your approach?	Y	N
Have you been looking for a way to rid yourself of your fear first, and then fly after you've become fearless?	Y	N
Do you tend to think it's not okay to feel afraid on an airplane?	Y	N
Do you try to suppress your fear?	Y	N
Do you try to hide your fear?	Y	N

The most effective form of treatment available for phobias is exposure treatment. As previously explained, it's based on the understanding that as people spend time feeling and facing their fear, it diminishes, so long as they don't fight it or flee it.

Common Misunderstandings About Exposure

1. You must wait for the day you feel fearless.

Even when people know that exposure is the best method for overcoming this fear, they often misunderstand what it means to do exposure work. They think (or hope) it means to go and engage in the phobic activity and not feel afraid. This is what leads people to postpone flying until they feel "ready." They're waiting for the day when they're fearless...and they never actually feel "ready" because they still feel afraid.

This is a common misconception among fearful fliers. When people sign up for my weekend workshop, they usually think about our flight as a test, an exercise in which they are expected to demonstrate that they are no longer afraid, and they wonder if they will be able to pass the test. It's not a test at all. It's a practice flight—practice experiencing and responding to your fear in the actual situation. That's the most effective practice there is, because it enables you to retrain your amygdala instead of continuing to argue with your cerebral cortex!

Exposure is aimed at the fear, rather than what triggers the fear. Exposure is not really aimed at the highway, for driving phobics; or the dog, for dog phobics; or the elevator, for elevator phobics. It's about going to the highway, the dog, or the elevator, because that's a good way to get the fear that's needed for the exposure. Exposure is practice with fear itself. It succeeds by helping your amygdala develop new memories and associations to flying.

2. You must put yourself in the feared situation, then fight off the fear.

Resisting and opposing your fear is the opposite of what you need in exposure practice. Exposure is about working *with* the symptoms of fear, not against them. When it comes time to do your practice flight, that will be the point of the flight—to fly with fear—and I'll show you how to handle that in Chapter 11.

Fly when you're afraid. That's how you will retrain your amygdala, how you'll get the practice accepting and coping with your fear. That's how you can gradually build your confidence.

Does that idea, flying while afraid, scare you? It probably does, but it's literally okay to fly while afraid. As long as you're a passenger!

If you're part of the crew—a pilot or a flight attendant—I agree you probably shouldn't be afraid, because it might interfere with your doing your job. But if you're a passenger, what is your job? You don't have one. You're just there to be moved from one location to another. You're baggage that breathes! So feeling afraid will not interfere with any important job you have on the airplane. You can bring whatever thoughts, emotions, and physical sensations that you happen to experience at the time. It's a come-as-you-are party! The TSA people will scrutinize your carry-on bags and maybe your shoes, but not your thoughts and feelings. Smoking will not be permitted on the flight, but feeling afraid will be allowed.

Wouldn't you feel more comfortable if you weren't afraid? Absolutely! If you could simply and easily shrug off your fears without aggravating them, that would be the way to go. This is what people hope to achieve with safety behaviors. But most safety behaviors make your fears more persistent, rather than eliminating them. You probably observed that in the previous chapter.

It's not so easy to simply discard your fears without aggravating them in the process. Fortunately, so long as you're in Group 3 or 4, you don't have to. What has the fear ever actually done to you? If you're like the other people in Groups 3 and 4, it's scared you into believing that, this time, unlike all the other times, you're really going to "lose it," or even lose your life. But then the plane landed and you went on about your business.

The fear has literally tricked you. You've been tricked into treating it like danger, when it's much more useful to treat it like discomfort. If you're in Group 3 or 4, your fear is a sign of discomfort, not danger. That's what makes it okay to feel afraid.

If you were able to let yourself fly while feeling afraid, would that amount to giving up? Absolutely not! What we know from the research and experience with exposure therapy, and what I know personally from my experience with hundreds of fearful fliers, is that the fear and anxiety gets relieved, over time, by exposure. Exposure therapy is not simply putting up with fear, or giving up the desire to feel calm. It's about retraining your amygdala, and working with fear in ways that naturally reduce it over time.

Maybe right now you're having a thought that says something like this: "Nothing terrible has happened so far, but what if it does?" You're experiencing anticipatory worry about flying. We'll take a look at that in Chapter 10.

This idea, that it's okay to feel afraid, might seem like a radical and unrealistic idea to you at this point. That's okay. We've already seen how our gut instincts in responding to this kind of fear tend to be wrong. But you don't need to assume anything here, or take this idea that it's okay to be afraid on faith and hope it's true. Let's take a look at how you've experienced the fear of flying when you've been on flights up to now by looking at the symptoms of fear you've experienced.

CHAPTER 8

Break the Fear Into Its Parts

. . . .

What symptoms of fear have you experienced on board past flights? It'll be helpful to break the fear down into its four different types.

Fearful Thoughts

The first symptom type is fearful thoughts. Scary thoughts about flying might include thoughts of crashing, losing control and loudly demanding that the plane land immediately, charging the cockpit, trying to open a door or window, dying of fright, going insane, being restrained by passengers and crew, and more. But *thoughts* don't actually involve your doing these things, or having these experiences. Thoughts consist of thinking about them, worrying about them, trying to figure out how to prevent them, and picturing them occurring as you sit there in your seat.

Thoughts are perhaps the trickiest of the symptoms. All of us tend to treat thoughts as particularly important parts of life. We literally live in thoughts the way a goldfish lives in water, and it's easy to assume that our thoughts are somehow like the view a submariner gets from looking through a periscope—an actual view of the real world.

Yet, walk down any crowded street and take a look at the people passing by. They're mostly having thoughts about the same topic you are—themselves. Most of our thoughts are about ourselves, not the world around us. Even when the topic seems to be something external to us—a plane, a restaurant, a movie star—we're always present in our own thoughts. It's often about how we're affected (or expect to be affected). It's not always about us, but it usually is.

As you'll see in Chapter 10, the anxious thoughts you have about flying are best understood as symptoms of nervousness. This is why you could be seated on an airplane, filled with fear and thinking that something terrible is about to happen, and notice that the other passengers don't seem to be bothered at all. It's because that thought you're having, of something terrible about to happen, is just a symptom of your nervousness. It's not about the plane, it's about you. It means "I'm nervous," the same way the symptom of sweaty palms means you're nervous.

Crashing is not okay, and neither is running amok on an airplane. But having nervous thoughts about those topics is okay.

We tend to think our thoughts are really important and accurate. But thoughts are just what the brain does, in the same way that digestion is what the stomach does. They're both organs with a function. Brains do thoughts, and stomachs do digestion. Sometimes when we're nervous, it affects those organs. The thoughts and the digestion we experience when we're nervous or afraid will be affected by that emotion, and they might not be as good as when we're feeling calm. It's good to know that and to take it into account when working with nervous thoughts. All thoughts are not created equal.

What scary thoughts do you usually experience as part of your fear?

Crashing dying

Negative Emotions

The second symptom type is negative emotions. The emotions you experience will, of course, include fear. But there are usually others. Shame, blame, and embarrassment are common emotional components of fear, based on the idea that it's odd, bad, and uncommon to experience this fear. Anger is a common component. Frustration and despair are also present when a person struggles with the fear of never doing any better with this problem.

What emotions do you experience as part of your fear?

panic / shame / despair

Physical Sensations

The third symptom type consists of a wide range of physical sensations while on board an aircraft. These might include a change in heart rate; labored breathing or hyperventilation; chest pain, tightness, or pressure; feeling dizzy or lightheaded; tingling and numbness in the extremities; stomach distress; urge to urinate; sweating; and more. These are physical symptoms of anxiety that are commonly associated with panic attacks.

What physical sensations do you experience as part of your fear?

sweating / nauseated / shaky

Involuntary Fearful Behaviors

The fourth symptom type is involuntary, or automatic, behaviors of fear. This is a very small category. It includes a small number of behaviors that you might find yourself doing while afraid. You probably don't intend to engage in these behaviors, they "just happen" without your specific intention. Crying is a good example, as is nail biting, drumming your fingers, jiggling your leg, shifting restlessly in your seat, and reflexively clutching the seat, the armrest, or the passenger next to you. Crying out various exclamations of fear, like "oh no!", is another example, as is a startle reflex to an unexpected sound or sensation.

Let me explain the difference between these involuntary behaviors and safety behaviors, which you listed in Chapter 6. Safety behaviors are actions you deliberately take in an effort to feel less afraid, actions that unfortunately lead you to feel more afraid and vulnerable over time. Examples include the use of tranquilizers and alcohol, wearing a lucky shirt, monitoring the faces of the crew for signs of concern, and pretending you're at home in your living room rather than on board an airplane. Safety behaviors are a very different class of behavior from the involuntary behaviors we're discussing now. The involuntary behaviors are symptoms; safety behaviors are efforts to prevent and stop the symptoms. It's important to stop engaging in safety behaviors, because they will maintain your fear of flying if you continue to engage in them. It's okay to continue experiencing the involuntary behaviors. All you need to do with involuntary fearful behaviors is accept and observe them.

With one exception. The exception is the various forms of dysfunctional breathing that often accompany moments of panic and high anxiety—labored, shallow chest breathing; hyperventilation; and holding your breath. This breathing is not a safety behavior, because people don't deliberately engage in it in an effort to feel less afraid. It's an involuntary behavior, but I want to treat it differently because it produces so many other physical symptoms and it's relatively easy to correct.

Dysfunctional breathing can produce a variety of strong physical symptoms of fear, like feeling light headed and dizzy, tingling in the extremities, chest tightness and heaviness, and increased heart rate. These symptoms, however scary and unpleasant they may seem, are not in any way harmful. However, they can easily distract you and "throw you off your game" as you do flying exposure. If you struggle with these physical symptoms, I think it's worthwhile to practice a good breathing exercise, and you'll find one in the next chapter.

Full disclosure: Not everyone agrees with me on this point. Some mental health professionals think you should just accept and observe the dysfunctional breathing the same as you do with all the other symptoms (except for the safety behaviors). I don't entirely disagree with their reasoning, and if you want to do it that way, I think that's okay. But my experience has been that people who struggle with short and shallow breathing, and the strong physical symptoms it can produce, find it easier to make progress when they learn how to relax their breathing, and I'll show you how to do that in Chapter 9.

To summarize, then, about how to handle the behavioral symptoms:

Involuntary behaviors: Simply observe and accept them, and note them on your Symptom Inventory (see Chapter 11).

Safety behaviors: Leave them behind when you travel. If and when they crop up, refrain and interrupt them.

Dysfunctional breathing: Do the belly breathing, or just observe and accept, your choice.

List your involuntary behaviors here:

clutching seat

shutting eyes

holding hand.

When you're done listing the four types of symptoms above—fearful thoughts, negative emotions, physical sensations, **and** involuntary fearful behaviors—you'll have listed most, if not all, of the symptoms you're likely to experience on board your practice flight. Be as thorough as you can in creating these lists. You'll use them in Chapter 11 to create a Symptom Inventory for use during your practice flight.

> When you evaluate your thought symptoms, remember that I'm not asking if what the thought describes or suggests would be dangerous. I'm asking if the simple act of having the thought is dangerous. It's the difference between an earthquake and a thought of an earthquake.

When you're done with your four symptoms lists, I'd like you to consider these questions.

Are there any symptoms on your lists that are dangerous?	**Y**	**N**
Any that are inexcusable and unforgivable?	**Y**	**N**
Any that will severely limit or trouble your life thereafter?	**Y**	**N**
Does it seem like a good trade to you to give up flying for the rest of your life, if that's what it takes to avoid these symptoms?	**Y**	**N**

As you review each of your symptoms, do they represent danger or discomfort?

_____

_____

_____

Paying a Price

If you have actually done something dangerous on a plane, come into conflict with the crew or the authorities, or experienced something dangerous, then you need to take that seriously and find a way to prevent that from happening again. It's important to prevent and protect against danger.

What about your symptoms that aren't dangerous, but are really uncomfortable? It would be nice to find a way to be rid of those symptoms so you could feel more comfortable on the flight. This is how I think about the belly breathing. Just be aware that the belly breathing is not saving your life or your sanity. It just helps you feel a little more comfortable and makes it easier for you to do the exposure work.

If, somehow, you could pay $5 to be rid of the rest of your symptoms of fear, that would definitely be worth it. That would be like a cheap upgrade to emotional first class.

Would you pay $50 to be free of your symptoms? An extra $50 on top of your airfare would probably still seem like a good deal.

How about $50,000? Now the price is probably getting too high. However, when you try hard to prevent and protect against your symptoms of fear, you're getting tricked into paying a price, a very high and dear price, one that you probably wouldn't choose to pay, deliberately and consciously. You're paying the price of restricting your freedom and mobility.

When you resist and try so hard to prevent feeling afraid, you get tricked into maintaining and strengthening your symptoms of fear. This is what happened to the businessman I cited in Chapter 3. He brought his lucky shirt, and gripped the armrest, and closed his eyes, and drank some vodka tonics in hopes of becoming unafraid. He tried so hard to rid himself of his symptoms of fear, only to find that his problem got worse rather than better. He would have been much better off to get rid of all those safety behaviors and instead work with AWARE (which I'll discuss on page 99) and the belly breathing.

Responding to a Counterintuitive Problem

If your new puppy gets off the leash and runs down the street, what's the best way to get that puppy back to safety?

You probably feel like running after that puppy. But you have two legs, and the puppy has four, so this is unlikely to go your way. When you chase that puppy, the puppy will enjoy the game of running away and play it harder. No, chasing an untrained puppy is not the way to go, as much as your instinct tells you to do it.

You could call to the puppy, tell it to come back. But this new puppy is untrained and will just enjoy the game of shout and run.

What's going to work best with this problem puppy? If you run away from the puppy, rather than toward, I bet that puppy will turn around and chase you, enjoying this new game of catch the owner. Then you can grab him, and everyone will be happy.

That runaway puppy is a counterintuitive problem. If you follow your intuition, your gut instinct of how to solve it, you'll probably make the problem worse. You have to do something very different to solve a counterintuitive problem.

The fear of flying is the mother of all counterintuitive problems.

Fortunately, there's a powerful and surprising rule of thumb about panic attacks and phobias, one you can put to good use in overcoming the fear of flying. This is the subject of the next chapter.

CHAPTER 9

The Rule of Opposites

....

Here's the background to the Rule of Opposites: Your gut instinct in responding to a panic attack is typically dead wrong. The instinctive response to a panic attack is to do something you hope will help, but that actually makes it worse. It's like a situation in which your compass is off by 180 degrees, pointing north but calling it south.

The reason your compass is reversed is because you're experiencing discomfort but treating it like danger. And what's good for discomfort (chill out and give it time to pass) is the opposite of what's good for danger (fight or flight). When people have a panic attack, they tense up the muscles of their legs and core when they would do better to let those muscles relax. They argue with their fearful thoughts when they would do better to humor those thoughts. They flee the scene when they would do better to hang out and let the fear gradually subside. They hold their breath when it would be much better to relax and breathe comfortably.

It's as if they've been sabotaged, tricked into responding in ways that will make them feel worse rather than better. And this applies, not only to people with Panic Disorder, but also to people with specific phobias in the moment when they encounter the object or location or activity they fear. It applies when a fearful flier gets frightened on an airplane.

Here's an example from my own life. There was a time when I worked at overcoming a fear of heights. During this time, whenever I found myself in San Francisco, I'd make it my business to walk across the Golden Gate Bridge. Now, if you're afraid of heights and looking to do some exposure practice with that fear, the Golden Gate is a great place to do it!

The first time I started walking there, I became extremely afraid and felt like I couldn't do it. I observed other people walking as if it were nothing—older people with canes and walkers, young kids on bicycles (not even walking their bicycles, but *riding them* on the bridge!), people walking their dogs (some of those dogs weren't even on a leash!)—and I realized they were all walking faster than me. I noticed that one of the things slowing me down was that I was literally dragging my heels. I was trying to keep my feet connected to the surface of the bridge at all times. It's hard to walk that way!

I immediately remembered the Rule of Opposites. I admit I wasn't so happy to remember it at first, but I went ahead and did what it suggested. I hopped. It was the world's shortest hop—it's probably in the *Guinness Book of World Records*—but it's hard to overestimate the positive effect it had on me at the time. It relaxed my body, because you can't hop and hold yourself all tight and tense at the same time. That felt good. It was a silly thing to do and made me laugh; that felt good. And, since there was a 10-foot fence on the side of the bridge, I was in no danger of falling off.

That's what I mean by the Rule of Opposites, finding small behaviors you engage in at a moment of high anxiety and fear and turning them on their head, literally doing the opposite.

So, the Rule of Opposites says you should do the opposite of your gut instinct when you panic. You can find your way home when your compass is off by 180 degrees, as long as you know it's pointing precisely in the wrong direction.

Deep Breathing

The rules of opposites is most apparent when people become anxious and feel short of breath, lightheaded, and dizzy. Is that a symptom you experience, either on board a plane or while worrying about a trip?

If it is, then I'd like you to try a breathing exercise now.

Maybe you've already heard so much about breathing that you're sick of it. If you've experienced a lot of panic attacks, you've probably been told, many times, "Take a deep breath!" And it hasn't helped. That's frustrating to a lot of people. The problem is, nobody ever tells you **how** to take this deep breath. And that's the key. So before you mutter "breathing, schmeething!" to yourself and skip to the next topic, give this deep breathing exercise a try. I think you'll find something different here.

Take a minute now, before you read any further. Recall a time when you felt short of breath, maybe unable to breathe, while on a plane or preparing to board. What did you do about it?

_____

People often try a variety of things hoping to influence their breathing—a cold drink of water, turning the fan to blow on your face, distraction—but I'd like you recall what you actually did or tried to do with your breath. What did you do with your breath?

_____

If your answer was that you took a deep breath (or tried to), then I'd like you to do the same thing now. First, put one hand on your chest, and one on your belly, right at your beltline. Use your hands to notice what muscles you use to do the breathing. Take that breath, the way you did it before, just once, before you read any further.

All done? What was that breath like? What muscles in what part of your body did you use to do the breathing? _____

_____

Here's what most people do in this situation when they're anxious and having trouble catching their breath. They strain to inhale, and even though they have the right idea of taking a deep breath, what they actually do is take a very labored shallow breath, from their chest. They pull that breath from their sternum, at the center of their chest, and raise their head and shoulders toward the ceiling as they do.

They don't actually take a deep breath. They take a labored, uncomfortable, shallow breath, one that tenses the muscles of their upper body. But, without giving it much review, they think of it as a deep breath, probably because they're putting so much effort into it.

It's not a deep breath. It's a tiny breath they try to force into the tops of their lungs, one that will make them more uncomfortable rather than less. What works better is the opposite of that, a gentle sigh or exhale that relaxes the muscles of your upper body and brings your shoulders down, followed by an inhale that's accomplished by pushing your belly out. Isn't that surprising? Your brain is screaming at you, "Take a deep breath!" And yes, that's a good idea; but first, it works better to give a breath away.

Exercise Instructions

Want to try it now? Follow these instructions.

1. Place one hand just above your beltline and the other on your chest, right over the breast-bone. You can use your hands as a simple biofeedback device. Your hands will tell you what part of your body, and what muscles, you are using to breathe.

2. Open your mouth and gently sigh, as if someone had just told you something really annoying. As you do, let your shoulders and the muscles of your upper body relax in a downward direction with the exhale. The point of the sigh is not to completely empty your lungs. It's just to relax the muscles of your upper body.

3. Close your mouth and pause for a few seconds.

4. Keep your mouth closed and inhale *slowly* through your nose by pushing your stomach out. The movement of your stomach precedes the inhalation by just the tiniest fraction of a second, because it's this motion that is pulling the air in. When you've inhaled as much air as you can comfortably (without throwing your upper body into it), just stop. You're finished with that inhale.

5. Pause. How long? You decide. I'm not going to give you a specific count, because everybody counts at a different rate, and everybody has different size lungs. Pause briefly for whatever time feels comfortable. However, be aware that when you breathe this way, you are taking larger breaths than you're used to. For this reason, it's necessary to *breathe more slowly than you're used to*. If you breathe at the same rate you use with your small, shallow breaths, you will probably feel a little lightheaded from over-breathing, and it might make you yawn. Neither is harmful. They're just signals to slow down. Follow them!

6. Open your mouth. Exhale through your mouth by pulling your belly in.

7. Pause.

8. Continue with steps 4 to 7.

Many people find it easier to learn from watching a demonstration, rather than just reading a set of instructions. You can find a video demonstration here: https://www.youtube.com/watch?v=eRIV2R3jzaQ

I'm not telling you anything new here. You used to breathe this way all the time, before you got away from it. If you want to see some world-class belly breathers, check out some newborns or young children. Their tummies go out and in as they breathe. That's how we're born to breathe.

The Rule of Opposites works for something as purely physical as breathing. Your instinct is to gulp air in, rapidly, from your chest. It will work better to do the opposite—to first gently exhale. Then you are in position to do what you wanted originally, to take that deep breath in comfortably from your belly.

The Rule of Opposites also works well with lots of other anxious responses on a plane.

Remember the businessman in Chapter 3, who gripped the armrest? What did that do? It didn't make him any safer, because the seatbelt was already holding him in far more effectively than he could with his forearms. It did, however, increase muscle tension and signal to his amygdala that something must be wrong. It promotes anxiety rather than reduces it! What would work better? Letting go of the armrest and getting used to relaxing your arms. The opposite of your gut instinct.

Fearful fliers often watch the faces of the crew for any sign of concern or trouble. What does this do? If people could do one simple check and then feel relief, that might be useful. But more typically they keep checking throughout the flight, the same way a dog phobic watches for a dog as he walks home from the train station. The constant checking makes them more, not less, nervous. The dog phobic doesn't feel any relief until he gets in the house, and the fearful flier doesn't feel relief until he gets off the plane. What would work better? Notice how you keep feeling the pull to examine the faces of the crew, have a chuckle about that, smile at them, and let your gaze turn to other items of interest, as well.

Or be playful and make a game of it. See if you can identify the crew member who's most likely to have a nervous breakdown before the plane lands!

The effect of the Rule of Opposites is even stronger when you consider how you may struggle to silence, disprove, and remove your fearful thoughts. Fearful fliers usually argue with their thoughts throughout the flight, hoping this will somehow make them more calm, only to end up more upset and tense from all the arguing. An argument with yourself is not an argument you're going to win.

What would work better than arguing with yourself? Well, what would be the opposite of that?

Simply put, humoring your thoughts would be the opposite of arguing with them, and that will work better for you in the long haul. I'll suggest some specific ways you can do this in Chapter 10.

The Rule of Opposites also applies to many of the symptoms people experience in the weeks before a scheduled flight, in the anticipatory stage. Some people will monitor the weather channel for weeks before their flight, hoping to find a guarantee that the weather will be perfect. It rarely is! And even if you do happen to see a perfect report, you have to keep checking back to see if it changes! The constant need to check, and the attempt to feel sure about something as changeable as the weather, makes the person more nervous rather than less. And all this monitoring is for nothing, because the airline has a team of people watching the weather, and they're not going to invite you into their planning meetings just because you watch the weather channel!

Go back and review your four lists of symptoms you experience on flights, the ones you made in Chapter 8. Write each of those fearful thoughts, negative emotions, physical sensations, and involuntary behaviors in the spaces below.

As you write each one, take a moment to remember what it's like to experience that symptom on an airplane, and recall how you react to it. What is your instinctive response when you experience these symptoms on an airplane? Write your instinctive response in the line below each symptom.

Symptoms and Responses

Fearful Thoughts

_____

_____

_____

_____

_____

_____

_____

Negative Emotions

_____

_____

_____

_____

_____

_____

_____

_____

Physical Sensations

_____

_____

_____

_____

_____

_____

_____

Involuntary Behaviors

_____

_____

_____

_____

_____

_____

_____

With each response you listed, ask yourself this question: Does this response make me more comfortable, or more anxious?

What does it mean when you find responses to your symptoms that lead you to feel more anxious, and more stuck, when you're just trying to help yourself feel better? It means that you took the bait of a counterintuitive problem and responded with an intuitive response. For example, sometimes people find themselves crying in response to their fear and try to hide this from others, only to feel more embarrassed and ashamed. They were hoping it would help to hide their crying but got the opposite result.

So it's okay if you cry, and there's probably no benefit to hiding or resisting it. People usually feel better after a cry. So bring tissues! We don't want the pilot to be crying, but you'll be a passenger, so that's okay.

You might also find some responses that do help you feel more comfortable in the moment, but have marked disadvantages in the long term. An alcoholic beverage will make most people feel more comfortable, but as they come to depend on this help, it enlarges, rather than shrinks, their troubles.

"The harder I try, the worse it gets." If that describes your history with the fear of flying, it's because you've been trying ways that actually do make it worse. It's not that you're an ineffective person. It's that you've been trying ineffective responses.

Make a list of the responses that seem to be ineffective and unhelpful for you. Consider what the Rule of Opposites has to say about more useful replacements for those ineffective responses. Perhaps, for instance, you're in the habit of closing your eyes during the flight, and come to recognize that this actually leads you to experience more doubt and fear as you wonder what's happening around you. Maybe the opposite action of looking around and letting yourself acclimate to that anxiety would be a good replacement.

Use the Rule of Opposites to identify possible replacements for each of the ineffective responses on your list.

REPLACEMENT RESPONSES

SYMPTOM	INEFFECTIVE RESPONSE	REPLACEMENT RESPONSE

CHAPTER 10

Anticipatory Worry

....

Picture a fisherman sitting on a pier, fishing and enjoying a lazy Sunday afternoon. What happens when a fish bites down onto a baited hook? The fisherman gets all excited, but what happens from the fish's perspective?

A fish that bites down onto a baited hook knows immediately that something is wrong, because the hook pierces its lip. That tells the fish this isn't the tasty morsel it expected. Somebody's trying to make a meal out of him. What does the fish do?

Most fish will swim as fast as they can, in a straight line away from the pier, hoping to get away. And maybe they will, if the hook is really loose. But this headlong rush away from the fisherman often places the fish in greater peril. The harder he swims away, the more securely the hook gets set in his mouth. And the fisherman will magnify this effect by tugging on the line to set it even more deeply.

The fish has encountered a counterintuitive problem. If it follows its gut instinct and flees, it's liable to end up in the frying pan tonight.

A more savvy fish, one that has survived previous encounters with fisherman and their hooks, is likely to respond in a counterintuitive way. This fish will probably swim right at the pier, to the spot where the line enters the water. This makes it more likely that the hook will get dislodged, because there's no tension on the line. And if it's still hooked when it reaches the pier, maybe it can get the line tangled in the pier and break free.

This is one smart fish! It knows what to do when it discovers that it's taken the bait. And it will be a lot less likely to take the bait next time it's offered.

What does this have to do with the fear of flying? Fearful fliers get baited, too. Your bait is different. You get hooked on "what if?" thoughts and other forms of fearful anticipation in the days and weeks before an upcoming flight. And how you respond to the bait will have a lot to say about whether your fear of flying increases or decreases over time.

What do you usually do when you find yourself hooked on these worrisome thoughts? How do you respond? You probably do something, react in some way that you hope will restore some calm to your mind. What do you do?

Take a few minutes to review your experience with fearful anticipatory thoughts, and list some of the ways you try to calm yourself.

_____

_____

_____

All done with your list? Now I'd like you to go back and rate the effectiveness of each of the responses you listed. Rate each one from zero to 100 percent in terms of how effective your response is in calming your thoughts so you can get on with the business of your day.

What I've observed with fearful fliers is that they tend to take their worry thoughts literally. A person who has thoughts about freaking out and charging the cockpit starts to wonder how she can prevent herself from doing that, and what will happen if she does it anyway. A person who has thoughts about crashing starts to think about getting off the plane while he still has a chance to avoid this ghastly fate.

These people have taken the bait the same way the fish did. The fish takes the bait, maybe a worm or a small fish on a hook, to be a nutritious morsel, and tries to swallow it. Fearful fliers take the bait of their worrisome thoughts to be important, accurate predictions of the future and try to figure out how to protect against those grim outcomes.

They've both been tricked. What the fish takes to be a meal is actually a trap. What the fearful flier takes to be a warning of some grim future event is actually nothing more than present nervousness. A fish that takes the bait and then flees the vicinity of the pier will probably make its situation worse by setting the hook more deeply. A fearful flier who mistakes the nervous thoughts for a threat and resists them will similarly make his situation worse by increasing, rather than decreasing, his anxiety.

Those worrisome thoughts and feelings are signs of discomfort, but the fearful flier treats them like danger. This is the principal reason that your efforts to calm and neutralize anxious thoughts about flying are generally so unhelpful. You get tricked into opposing, arguing with, and trying to silence your worrisome thoughts in ways that will generally make the thoughts more persistent and upsetting. You're putting out fires with gasoline!

Are You Taking the Anxiety Bait?

How successful are your usual efforts at calming your thoughts? If you're like most fearful fliers, they're probably not very effective. You'll probably find better ways to respond to your anticipatory worries by recalling the Rule of Opposites: What's good for discomfort is generally the opposite of what's good for danger. What may surprise you is that this is even effective with thoughts. The key is to become more clearly aware when you're having a thought that's just anxiety bait.

A fish might be able to identify bait by the presence of the fishing line or the glint of the hook. You can do something similar. Your bait of worrisome thoughts almost always begins with the words "what if?" The rest of the sentence is whatever catastrophe you fear: freaking out, acting crazy, crashing, dying of a heart attack, and so on. Your bait can be diagrammed this way:

What if... _____? (Insert any catastrophe here.)

What do the words "what if" mean? What meaning do they add to the full sentence?

_____

_____

Maybe you wrote down that they mean possibilities. That's part of it, but when is the last time you had this thought: "What if I meet a beautiful stranger on the plane and we fall in love and run away to a glorious life on a Pacific island?"

You probably haven't been having that thought so often. These "what if" thoughts are always about something bad. And they're about something bad that isn't happening now. Are these bad things possible? Yes, mostly, but what isn't possible? Anything is possible in the future, and simply listing bad possibilities isn't a good way of forecasting the future. So, what do the words "what if" really mean here?

I think they mean "let's pretend." The entire "what if" sentence is an invitation. "Here's something terrible that isn't happening now, and why don't you go ahead and pretend that it is?"

That doesn't sound so attractive, does it? And if you dangled an empty fish hook in front of a fish with nothing to disguise it, it probably wouldn't attract too many fish, either. The fishhook has to be disguised with interesting stuff that looks like tasty food in order to get the fish to take the bait. Your worry about improbable bad things has to be disguised in order to get you to take the bait. That disguise is usually the words "what if?"

The "what if" part of the worry thought tells you all you need to know. You're nervous and having unpleasant thoughts that pretend bad things will happen in the future. Just because these symptoms of nervousness are thoughts doesn't make them any more accurate, or important, or threatening. They mean "I'm nervous" the same way sweaty palms mean "I'm nervous." Sweaty palms don't mean "I'm losing all my bodily fluids" or "I'm at risk of dehydration." They simply mean "I'm nervous," and that's all these anticipatory thoughts mean.

Years ago, before there was a "no call" law that restricted telemarketers from calling you at home with unwanted solicitations, something often happened in homes across America. The phone would ring, usually at dinner, and when you answered it, the caller would say something like, "I have some free magazines for you!" If you heard that statement and took it to mean that you were getting a free gift, then you would probably be conned into buying some things you didn't really want or need. On the other hand, if you recognized it as a sales call, then you would probably be in position to handle it the way you wanted.

These "what if" thoughts about your flights are similar sucker bait. They mean "here's some awful event that isn't happening now, why don't you go ahead and pretend that it is?"

The fact that these "what if" thoughts are subliminal, that they slip through your mind without you even noticing their presence, gives them more power. You don't notice the part of the thought that says, "Here's something terrible that isn't happening now but why don't you pretend that it is!" You just notice the catastrophe clause, the description of a terrible feared disaster and take that as bad news rather than a simple sign of you being nervous.

It's okay to be nervous, particularly since you will only be a passenger on this flight. In fact, that's the whole point of your practice flight, to get nervous! It's okay for passengers to feel nervous. It's not going to affect the flight. It'll be helpful if you can become more aware of these thoughts in the moment, to catch them in the act, and thereby be less likely to take the bait.

Here's a way you can do that.

Go to the store and buy a couple of little plastic boxes of Tic Tacs. They come 60 to the box. Carry a box with you at all times, and get into this habit: Each time you notice the "what if" thought or catch yourself saying "what if" about flying, open up your box and take a mint out. You can eat it, or you can flick it into the trash, that doesn't matter. You'll be using the boxes of Tic Tacs as a way to count how many such thoughts you have in a day or a week. The count itself might be interesting—the number will probably be higher than you imagine. But the number isn't that important itself, it's just a means to an end. You can use the counting of Tic Tacs to help you get better at catching yourself in the act when you have these "what if" thoughts, and this way you will get fooled less often.

These "what if" thoughts are like a red flag to a bull. The bull sees it, charges, and usually gets stabbed to death. You hear these "what if" thoughts, take them seriously, and get upset and afraid. We can't train the bull to respond to the red flag by laying down and eating daisies, but you can use Tic Tacs to train yourself to notice, and respond differently, to your "what if" thoughts.

It'll be well worth your effort!

What's Good for Nervousness?

It helps to treat nervousness as the discomfort it is, and it hurts to treat nervousness as a danger. In a very real sense, it's okay to be nervous, and so our guiding rule of thumb is to expect and accept that you will be nervous as you go about your project of overcoming the fear of flying.

It's very common for fearful fliers to hope that they won't get afraid when they try to resume flying. This is the kind of thing that gives hoping a bad name! It's unhelpful to hope this way, and I suggest you do the opposite: Expect that you will get afraid as you start flying again, and accept that fear as best you can, rather than resist it. If you were afraid of dogs and were scheduled to go visit a dog, it would only be natural for you to experience fear. It's the same with the fear of flying. Show up for the fear and go through the steps I'm describing here and in Chapter 12.

It is also more useful to respond to the anticipatory thoughts as they are—symptoms of being nervous—rather than getting embroiled in the content of your worries. The content doesn't really matter! This is what the presence of the "what if" clause tells you; it's *pretending* to know something bad about the future. You're not facing a threat around you, you're facing a fear within you. And, since you're only going to be a passenger on the airplane, it's okay to be afraid.

What Distraction Tells You

At this point, some readers will have had the thought, "But what if it does come true?" Did you have that thought? That's the bait!

You'll get more evidence of this—that you're up against a fear rather than a threat—when you look at the ways you've been trying to handle it. Do you try to distract yourself from your anxious thoughts? Most fearful fliers do, using books, movies, crossword puzzles, mobile phones, and more in an effort to distract themselves from the fact that they're on an airplane. It's common for fearful fliers to close their eyes and try not to notice, or remember, where they are. Distraction is a very common response.

What does it tell you about a problem you face if your instinct is to distract yourself? Give that a little thought. What kinds of problems do we typically try to distract from?

Maybe you're not so sure what I'm getting at here, so let me ask another question. If you see a large, hostile dog charging toward you, growling, fur back, clearly meaning to rip you from limb from limb, how likely are you to distract yourself by humming a little tune?

Not so likely, right? You wouldn't be distracting yourself at all. You'd be focused like a laser on that dog, looking for something, like a stick, a fence you could hop, or the dog's owner, that could protect you.

So, what does it tell you about a problem if your response is to try to distract yourself? It tells you that the chips are not down. It tells you that you're not in present danger; you're just having unpleasant, worrisome thoughts.

What does the fact that you're having these worrisome thoughts tell you? Let me ask you this: If you had a dog phobia and feared being bitten, when would you ever have the thought "what if a dog bites me?" _____

_____

You might suppose that you wouldn't have the thought when there are no dogs around. But a person with a strong phobia wouldn't trust that. He'd be wondering when, and from which direction, a dog will suddenly appear! He'd be having plenty of those thoughts when he doesn't see any dog. (And you probably experience the same thing, having fearful thoughts of flying when you don't even have a specific trip planned.)

When will he absolutely not have any of those thoughts? Only when a dog is attacking him. He'll be too busy trying to defend himself to pay any attention to thoughts at all. He'll only be paying attention to arms, legs, paws, teeth, sticks, and so on.

Worrying is a leisure-time activity. We only engage in it when we don't have something really important to do, in the present, and in the environment around us.

So, what does it really indicate when you're having all of these worrisome thoughts about flying? It means there's nothing you need to do to make yourself safe right now; you're already as safe as you can be. When you actually face a clear and present danger, you don't worry; you do what you can to protect yourself.

Perhaps you've listed distracting yourself as one of the ways you try to soothe the worrisome thoughts. If distraction actually helped you to feel better, then it would probably be okay. But for most fearful fliers, it seems to make things worse. They keep reading and rereading the same couple of pages, or keep watching the movie without comprehending the action, because trying to deliberately distract yourself or control your thoughts actually works pretty poorly.

Most people find that the harder they try to distract themselves, the more persistent their worries become. That's certainly what those people who keep trying thought stopping find as they snap rubber bands against their wrist and tell themselves to stop. They're still having the scary thoughts, and now their wrist hurts as well!

What's the opposite of distraction? Observation. So, here's a useful task. Make a list of all your usual suspect thoughts, all the anticipatory "what if" thoughts you expect to experience in the week or two before your practice flight.

Does that idea go against the grain for you? If it does, that's another sign that you're on the right track now, doing the opposite of your gut instinct. It's counterintuitive. That's what you need!

If you're willing, go a little further and make that list of all the worrisome and fearful thoughts you think you might conceivably experience in the days and weeks before your practice flight. Let your imagination run, and make your list as broad and inclusive as you can.

_____

_____

_____

_____

_____

_____

_____

_____

Did you find that you're a little fearful of writing out your fearful thoughts? Did it seem to you that this might somehow make the feared events more likely to occur? It's very common to have this kind of superstitious thought, that somehow what you think, or what you write, will change the future.

Are you concerned that your thoughts can somehow alter the future? Thoughts can sometimes spur a person to action that can influence events. A person might have the idea to change careers and then begin to do things that can make that happen. But that's very different from the idea that thoughts alone can influence the future.

Did you hesitate to write this list because you thought it might change your future for the worse? Check this out with a brief experiment.

Take three minutes and really concentrate on the thought that tomorrow, someone you know will tell you she's pregnant. See how you do.

Sooner or later, I suppose, that could happen, but I don't think that will happen because of your thoughts. Do you? The thought that your thoughts will shape the future is probably just another nervous thought.

Self-Disclosure Over Secrecy

Fearful fliers often try to hide their fear, to keep it a secret. What's the opposite of secrecy? Self-disclosure! Rather than hoping to keep your fear a secret, mention the fact that you're a fearful flier to the flight attendant who greets you as you board the airplane. This is not because you need them to do something, or even that there's something important that they can do for you. It's to help you be less concerned with hiding your secret, because trying to keep your fear a secret naturally requires that you remain on guard, watching for any sign of nervousness so that you can seek to suppress and hide it. What happens when you try to suppress a fear? You get the same result you get if you try to stop hearing a song that got stuck in your head. It becomes more persistent and repetitive!

Arguing with Yourself

Fearful fliers get into a confrontational stance with their worrisome thoughts. They argue with themselves in a variety of ways. Quietly or loudly, calmly or angrily, they disagree, try to persuade, and hope to have the last word.

This might be useful when you argue with others. But when you argue with yourself, this is not an argument you're going to win. Or lose, for that matter. It's more like an argument that will simmer and continue, because when you argue with yourself, it's a pretty even match, you against you.

Want to try an experiment? Take two minutes and don't think of an airplane. Don't picture one taking off. Don't imagine the view of people sitting in crowded rows, waiting to take off. Don't hear the sound of the door being closed or the pilot announcing takeoff. Tell yourself it's stupid to have these thoughts. Tell yourself to stop it! Keep flying out of your mind for two minutes.

How did you do? If you're like most fearful fliers, not so well.

It's a tricky thing, when you try to change your thoughts. You can change your clothes, and the clothes you threw into the hamper are not going to slither out of the hamper and crawl back onto your body. But when you try to change your thoughts, the thoughts you hoped to discard or correct are likely to reenter your mind, again and again, even as you try to discard them.

Cognitive Restructuring

What else do people do in their efforts to get rid of the scary thoughts?

They often try some form of cognitive restructuring, in which they look for the errors in their thinking, and correct them. A person who always fears that his plane will crash might say to himself, "I always have that thought! That's me doing some fortune telling, thinking that I can predict the future! I can't actually predict the future!" This is a traditional part of cognitive behavioral therapy. Its intent is to allow you to change your thoughts to thoughts that are more realistic, that have more evidence behind them.

My experience with cognitive restructuring is that fearful fliers try real hard to make it work, but often find that the unwelcome and irrational thoughts keep coming back. If you want to do cognitive restructuring and find that it helps you to dismiss the unwelcome worrisome thoughts, that's good. But if you find that, 15 minutes later, you're still stuck there in the same place, struggling to clear your mind of these thoughts, then consider trying a different method, one that involves acceptance rather than restructuring.

Worry Appointments

Deliberately allowing yourself to have the thoughts, rather than trying to prevent them, would be a good opposite. Humoring the thoughts, rather than resisting them, would be a good opposite. Here's how you can do this.

In the week or two before a flight, schedule some specific times to worry about flying. Is that the opposite of what you usually try? It probably is. Schedule two times daily, 10 minutes each, when you can be alone and have the privacy to worry and do nothing else. You're not listening to music, driving, riding a bus, having lunch, walking the dog, or anything else. No multitasking! You're just worrying, in the traditional way, repeatedly asking yourself lots of "what if" questions about the outcomes you fear.

What if... I freak out?

What if... I go crazy?

What if... We crash?

What if... I charge the cockpit?

What if... They throw me on the floor and tie me up?

What if... My family sees me on the nightly news?

What if... _____?
(fill in your particular fears here)

You can use the list of anticipatory worries you made earlier in this chapter as material for your worry appointments. Fill the 10 minutes with worry and no problem solving, no distracting, no reassuring. Make no effort to relieve the worry. Just keep repeating your worries for 10 minutes. Do this worrying out loud and in front of a mirror, so you can hear yourself worrying and see yourself worrying.

Sounds peculiar, yes? This is probably the complete opposite of how you usually try to head off your anticipatory worry. But what do you have to show for your usual efforts? How did you do with the experiment a couple of minutes ago, trying not to think of airplanes? If you're like most fearful fliers, you haven't gotten anything good from your efforts to oppose your worry thoughts. So, try something very different!

Why would anyone do this? The real benefit from worry appointments is that you're likely to develop a good ability to postpone your worries to your next scheduled appointment. This will help you sweep relatively clear portions of your day that used to be frequently interrupted by worry. If you find yourself worrying about flying in between your scheduled worry appointments, you can stop and offer yourself a choice: postpone your worrying until your next worry appointment, or do an additional one right now. And, if you do an extra one without the usual privacy, it's okay to skip the worrying aloud, and the mirror.

We know that trying to simply stop worrying usually has the opposite effect. However, the acceptance that's inherent in worry appointments will probably greatly increase your ability to postpone worry, provided that you are faithfully keeping your appointments to worry. If you try to fool yourself, if you try to postpone to the next appointment, but then don't keep the appointment to worry, you probably won't benefit from this.

Try that for a week or so and see what kind of effect it has on your ongoing anticipatory worry about flying.

What will you do with the anxiety you feel on your practice flight? We'll cover that in the next chapter.

CHAPTER 11

Handling Fear on Board the Plane

. . . .

Now, let's look at how you can respond to the fear you feel on board your practice flight. I hope it's no surprise to you that this seems really scary. Keep in mind that this is precisely why you're doing it—to practice with the fear so as to reduce your fear of becoming afraid over time. This is how you'll regain the ability to fly wherever you want!

Let's start with a reminder of your role on the flight: *You're a passenger*. There's nothing you need to control or make happen. Your role is to hang out and wait for the vehicle to get to your destination. As with any other passive task, you're liable to experience a variety of thoughts and feelings, and your mission is to practice having them today with as little resistance as possible.

What Did You Come Here For?

You'll probably hear this question in your automatic thoughts the day of your practice flight, maybe repeatedly, so let's run through the answer.

Why are you taking this trip? You don't have any business to conduct at your destination. You're probably not even going to leave the airport to go into town. And no one will come out to meet you, either. When you arrive, you'll turn around and go back home. So, what are you going there for?

You're literally going for the fear. This is how you can retrain your amygdala. You'll practice a new response, one in which you cease resisting the fear and anxiety in order to let it fade from your life. This flight will not do it all, but it will be one big step in a series of steps you can take to overcome the fear of flying and regain your ability to travel freely.

Be prepared to catch yourself in the act of expecting, or hoping, that you'll feel comfortable or at peace while on your practice flight. That will come on later flights, but for now, since you're a fearful flier, expect to feel afraid, with all its attendant discomforts. That will be your overall application of the Rule of Opposites—expecting and allowing yourself to feel anxious, rather than hoping, or struggling, to feel calm.

Let's think about how this will go.

The Day Before

Prepare your Symptom Inventory Form so you have it ready to go. Take the four lists of symptoms you developed in Chapter 8 and, when you're satisfied they're as complete as possible, list the symptoms on the two Symptom Inventory Forms in the appendix of this book.

Complete your Replacement Response list in Chapter 9, if you haven't yet done so.

The Night Before

Will you sleep well the night before your flight? Maybe, but it's not very likely. Naturally you will feel anxious, and that's likely to interfere with your sleep.

People often think they need to do something about that, such as work out so hard that they get tired, go to bed early (or late), take a sleeping pill or an alcoholic beverage, and so on. I don't think it's necessary to take any particular steps. If you were part of the crew, well, we'd like the crew to be well-rested, because they have a job to do. In fact, they have rules about that. But what's your job going to be? To sit and get afraid, and practice responding to those emotions in an accepting way. You don't need to be well-rested for that.

Don't make extraordinary efforts to sleep. Go to bed at your usual hour. Take a little time to do a deep breathing exercise or some meditation to make it a little easier to fall asleep, and then let whatever happens, happen. Recognize that you'll be nervous ahead of time, and be tolerant if you have trouble sleeping. It's not going to matter in the long term.

Expect to Feel Afraid

Let's consider how you can relate to the fear you feel. Follow some steps that will help you to accept, rather than oppose and resist, the fear. Now you're thoroughly acting on the Rule of Opposites, doing the opposite of your gut instinct.

On Arriving

Give yourself a reasonable amount of time to arrive at the airport. Many fearful fliers prefer to arrive at the last minute, so they have as little time as possible to hang around the gate and be nervous. But this kind of rushing creates its own anxieties. Consult your airline's website for suggestions about when to arrive at the airport, and follow their recommendation.

On Boarding

Most airlines will have you board in a planned order. Many fearful fliers prefer to wait in the gate until the very last moment before boarding the plane and taking their seat, but I don't recommend that, because it usually creates additional anxiety. You're already expecting to get afraid on this flight, right? That's why you're taking this trip to begin with! So go ahead and board in the order suggested by the airline, take your seat, and start practicing with the fear you feel.

Sometimes people try to cope with their anticipatory anxiety in the days before a flight by telling themselves they haven't made a final decision yet, and they'll decide whether or not to make this trip when they get to the airport. I don't recommend this because it increases the chance that you won't go. You won't have any new information that day on which to make a different decision. You'll just have stronger fear, which is the reason you planned this trip in the first place.

By the time you get to the airport, you have already made a lot of earlier decisions: to plan a practice flight, to buy the tickets, to travel alone or with a companion, to prepare your plans for how to handle your fear, and so on. You had good reasons for making those decisions. It's better to stay with all the decisions you've already made and just get on the plane when it's time, knowing that this is what you have already planned. No need to make any more decisions once you get to the airport. You don't need to work your brain at this point—just your feet.

However, if you do find yourself struggling at the last minute with a decision to board or not to board, here's what I suggest. Ask yourself when you need to feel better. If you need to feel better immediately, then you can leave. You'll start feeling better as soon as you turn toward the exit. Be aware, though, that the feeling won't last. You'll likely start feeling disappointed and upset with yourself by the time you get to the parking lot, and even more so by the time you get home. It won't be a fun night.

On the other hand, if you feel like you can wait a few hours to get that good feeling, then float with your fear and board the plane. That feels scary, of course, and that's exactly why you arranged this practice flight. You'll feel really good that night, when you get home after doing your practice flight, and that good feeling will last a lot longer.

A few minutes before you line up to board, start graphing your fear level on the "Outbound" graph sheet in the appendix. Thereafter, graph your level of anxiety, from 0 to 100, every 10 minutes during the flight. There's a second sheet for the return flight in the appendix.

Say hello to the crew member who greets you as you board, mention that you're afraid of flying (show them this book if you like!), smile, and invite the crew member to stop back and say hello during the flight if possible. There isn't anything you need this person to do, nor is there anything they can do that will immediately remove your fear. However, it's worth having this brief conversation with the flight attendant in order to help you stay away from trying to hide your fear. You don't need to hide it; it affects millions of people, and you're just one of them.

Once you're in your seat, review the materials in the appendix to remind yourself of the observational tasks you'll complete during your flights, and keep the book handy. Depending on how you feel right now, you might simply sit and talk with your companion, if you brought one; introduce yourself to whoever else is sitting in the row with you, and if you're willing, mention that you're afraid of flying; or do a few minutes of deep breathing. The fact that you have this book with you on the flight might be another way to break any secrecy about your fear, and set the stage for a brief conversation about it with a flight attendant or a fellow passenger, if you wish.

The AWARE Steps

Here's a five-step process you can use during the flight to guide your responses to the fear you feel. This is adapted from the excellent book *Anxiety Disorders and Phobias: A Cognitive Perspective*, by Beck, Emery, and Greenberg. These are steps that you can follow as often as you feel the need, whenever you're uncomfortably anxious and tempted to resist it.

A: Acknowledge and Accept

W: Wait and Watch

A: Act

R: Repeat

E: End

Acknowledge and Accept

ACKNOWLEDGE YOUR SYMPTOMS

The first part of this step involves you noticing that you're having various symptoms of fear—scary thoughts, physical sensations, and strong emotions. Ordinarily you might try to distract yourself or avoid noticing that you feel afraid, but not today, because you've come on board a flight for the express purpose of practicing with these feelings. You neither like them, nor do you deserve them, but here they are, and today is a day when you get to practice responding differently.

When you first feel a wave of fear, you might notice this question in your mind: "Oh, no, what did I come here for?"

Be ready with the answer. The answer to this question is: "These miserable feelings are what I came here for!" You've come to practice, rather than protect.

ACCEPT YOUR FEAR

The second part of this step involves you accepting the fact that you are afraid. It's okay to be afraid, and this is why you've come today. Ordinarily, you might grab the armrest, close your eyes and pretend you're home, drink a beer, ask God to intervene, cuddle with your support animal, tell yourself to stop feeling the way you do, argue with your fearful thoughts, or any and all of the safety behaviors that you listed in Chapter 6. But not today, because you've come on board a flight for the purpose of practicing with these symptoms.

Today, you've come on board the plane so you can allow yourself to feel afraid with as little struggle and resistance of the fear as possible. It's okay to feel afraid. You don't need to struggle to "get through" the flight. You just need to sit, observe your fear in its various forms, and allow the thoughts and feelings to come and go. Treat the symptoms of fear the way you might treat a headache. You don't like a headache, either, but you probably don't bang your head against the wall in an effort to make it go away. You probably notice the feelings of pain and reluctantly accept them, engage in whatever activities you do while the headache lasts, and give it some time to pass. It helps knowing that the headache will pass, and so will the fear.

It's easy to forget that the fear will pass. When you're very afraid, it can seem like it will last forever, that you're stuck in time like a bug in amber. But time continues to tick into the future, and the fear will pass.

Speaking of which, do you watch the passage of time, or follow the progress of the airplane on some electronic monitor, hoping to feel better by noticing that a few minutes or a few miles have already gone by? I used to watch the clock in some dull classes, and nothing made them seem longer than clock watching. Better to let that go!

IT'S NOT A TRAP!

The big moment most fearful fliers focus on is when the crew shuts the door and announces that the flight is going forward. This is why so many fearful fliers want to wait to board the plane until the last possible moment, because they suffer such agony sitting there, wondering when the door will close and whether they should run out while they still have a chance. They think of the plane as a trap when the door closes.

Of course, it's a good thing to close the door before a flight, just like you close the doors of your car before you drive off. It's much safer flying with the door closed! People get very upset as they struggle with their thoughts about the door being closed. They have all kinds of thoughts—of being trapped, of being unable to leave, and so on.

It's certainly true that you can't leave the plane while in midair. But this isn't because anyone wants to trap or confine you. This is because the safest place to be at the moment is inside the airplane! A trap is a situation imposed upon someone or something, typically a hunted animal, because someone wants to kill it.

People who fear driving on highways frequently experience the same thought, worrying about being trapped in a traffic jam. You're not trapped in a traffic jam or in an airplane. You're inconvenienced. You have to wait until the vehicle arrives at its destination. If you think you're trapped on an airplane, try staying on board after the plane lands and see what happens!

So, you don't have the reality of a trap, but you will have your own scary movie of a trap. That's okay. That's just another way of feeling afraid, and it's okay to feel afraid on the plane. Make sure those thoughts about being trapped are on your Symptom Inventory Forms (below) and refrain from arguing with them.

I worked with a fearful flier who had only been able to fly one time in more than a decade. And that flight was…a skydiving lesson! Her fear of the door being shut had kept her from flying for years. She was able to board the skydiving flight because she knew at some point, the door would open and she would be able to jump out!

It worked for her! But I think my method is easier.

Wait and Watch

WAIT

The fundamental task of a passenger is to wait. Wait for what? Wait for the vehicle to arrive at your destination, so you can get on with your day. The airplane is basically a waiting room.

Fearful fliers often find waiting uncomfortable, especially in an age when extreme multitasking has become the norm.

So, this is a waiting room for you. The challenge of a long stay in a waiting room is to work with the discomforts it imposes—the crowding, the quality of the furniture, the necessity to be away from your own sources of recreation and activity—without getting more frustrated, unhappy, or anxious than you have to.

Your stay in the waiting room (your trip on the airplane) is not the goal in and of itself. It's just a means to an end. There's someplace else you want to be, and this is a fast way to get there. The purpose of most trips is not the flying, it's what you plan to do once you arrive elsewhere. You will probably arrange to fly in circumstances that aren't nearly as nice and comfortable as the hotel you might book at your destination. Your time in, activity at, and enjoyment of the destination is the true purpose of most trips. The time on the airplane, not so much. So, today, you want to get some practice at just hanging out in the waiting room and taking a more accepting attitude toward it.

WATCH

Watch what? Watch yourself, and particularly pay attention to the role that you take on. When you get anxious on the airplane, you can either relate to the anxiety as an observer or a victim. An observer will notice the various symptoms with interest, take notes, and take a dispassionate attitude toward the discomforts experienced. A victim will seek to fight or avoid the symptoms. Your gut instinct will probably be to take the role of victim and respond with fight or flight. As you notice yourself getting caught up in the victim role, interrupt that and get back into the role of observer.

Use the following observational tools to help you stay in the role of observer whenever you feel restless or anxious. Copies of each of these tools are in the appendix at the end of this book. You can also discuss your observations in the moment with your travel companion, if you have one.

Anxiety Graph: Use the blank Graph Forms in the appendix to graph your anxiety level during the flight, at 10-minute intervals, on both legs of the trip. Start just before you board, and continue to do this throughout each flight until you leave the aircraft and arrive in the gate area.

Symptom Inventory: Hopefully you completed these forms the day before your practice flight so they're ready to go. But if not, then take the four lists of symptoms you developed in Chapter 8 and list the symptoms on the two Symptom Inventory Forms in the appendix of this book. Throughout the flights, each time you experience one of the symptoms in any category, put another *x* mark in one of the spaces to the right of the symptom name. In this way, you'll keep a count of how many times you experience each symptom.

You're keeping a count of how many times you experience each symptom, but the totals are not what's most important. Counting the symptoms is mostly a means to an end. The real payoff from doing this is it helps to put you squarely in the role of observer and counters any tendency to try to distract from or ignore the symptoms. It's another way to do the Rule of Opposites. Prepare two of these before your travel day, so you have one for each leg of the trip.

Panic Journals: From time to time during the flight, you are likely to feel extremely afraid and experience a panic attack. Stay with the AWARE steps, because they are the best response to a panic attack and will help you simply ride it out and give it time to pass. In addition, fill out the Panic Journal in the appendix. This is a version of the Panic Journal found in my *Panic Attacks Workbook*, modified to fit the flying experience.

Act

There isn't much to do on an airplane as a passenger, and so there isn't much action one needs to take. The essence of the passenger role is simply hanging out while waiting for the vehicle to arrive at your destination. However, there are a few things you can do to help you stay centered in your role of passenger.

When you experience any of the symptoms on your Replacement Response List in Chapter 9, experiment with using the replacement responses you identified on that list after noting the symptom on your Symptom Inventory.

Practice the belly breathing instructions in Chapter 9 when you feel your breathing is labored, or whenever you experience symptoms associated with labored breathing, such as light-headedness or dizziness; increased heart rate; tingling and numbness in the toes, fingers, and scalp; and tightness or heaviness in the chest. None of these sensations are dangerous. However, it will be easier for you to stay on track with your exposure practice if you relax your breathing in the manner described in Chapter 9 whenever you find yourself experiencing these symptoms. The belly breathing instructions described in Chapter 9 are not a silver bullet. They will not save you, because you're not in danger and don't need saving. However, they will help you respond more adaptively to the physical symptoms listed above, and help keep you from taking the bait and struggling against your anxiety symptoms.

You'll probably have a lot of "what if" thoughts that keep popping into your mind. You'll be keeping count of those on your Symptom Inventory Form, along with all the other symptoms. You might also find it helpful to practice responding in a playful way, rather than a resistant way. Did you find the "bad German accent" exercise in Chapter 5 useful? Here are some other ways to worry more playfully.

Make a haiku of your worries. Haiku is a form of traditional Japanese poetry, consisting of three unrhymed lines. The first line has five syllables, the second has seven, and the third has five. There's a lot more to haiku, but this is good enough for our purposes.

Here's an example of a haiku from a member of my workshop:

> *We're up in the air*
> *I want to open the door*
> *Get the duct tape out!*

The nice thing about creating a haiku of your worries is that it embodies acceptance. You're not resisting or denying or ignoring the thoughts at all. You're just playing with them. It's okay to play with thoughts!

Create a limerick. If haiku's not your style, maybe you'd enjoy converting your worries into a limerick. A limerick is a poem of five lines. The first, second, and fifth lines consist of seven to ten syllables each, must rhyme together, and have the same rhythm. The third and fourth lines consists of five to seven syllables each, must rhyme together, and have the same rhythm. (It sounds more complicated than it is!).

Here's an example of a limerick from a client:

> *There once was a gal from Belaire*
> *Who said I can't fly through the air!*
> *She opened the door*
> *Got thrown down on the floor*
> *And now she's in jail, who knows where!*

Worry in another language. Are you bilingual? Or even if you're not, did you ever study a foreign language in high school or college, however briefly? If so, you can do your worrying in your weaker language while you're on the plane. If you'd find it helpful, bring a bilingual dictionary to help you with this.

Just as with the poetry, you're not changing the subject or trying to get rid of the worries in any way. You're just transforming them, translating them into a different language. Still, it tends to change your reaction when you wrestle with issues such as how to say "turbulence" in German.

If you know nothing of any foreign languages at all, you can always use Pig Latin.

Sometimes people ask me if this is a form of distraction. No, it's not a distraction at all, because you're continuing to focus on the content of your worries, even as you create a poem or a translation. The subject matter remains the same. However, I think you'll find that it does have a beneficial effect on your emotional reactions to these thought symptoms.

What other actions can you take? You can get up and take a short walk to the rear of the plane, and use the bathroom if you want. You can talk to a flight attendant or a nearby passenger. You can converse with your support companion. You can use your belly breathing to gently relax your upper body, and observe your anxious thoughts with a more relaxed body. You can do some small stretches in your seat, perhaps tensing and relaxing major muscle groups.

None of these actions are essential. All that is really required of a passenger is to sit and wait for the vehicle to arrive. However, most passengers don't sit rigidly in their seat for the entire trip, and you don't need to, either. It's fine to use some of these as you get used to flying again, if you feel the need. As you take more trips, plan on reducing your reliance on these kinds of actions to the point where you can simply sit there and be bored with the rest of the passengers.

What about reading, watching a video, doing puzzles, and so on? I usually suggest fearful fliers leave those at home for their first practice flight. This is because you're so likely to try to lean on those activities as distractions, and the harder you try to distract yourself, the more of a counterproductive struggle it becomes. It's so common for people to read and reread the first couple of pages of a novel, because they can't really focus on it. Later, as you accumulate more practice with flying, you can begin to bring those items with you again.

Repeat

R stands for repeat. It's there to remind you that you may start to feel a little better as you use the AWARE steps, and then find another upsurge in fear. That's okay, just take it from the top, and go through the steps again. If we didn't have repeat in there, you might think something has gone wrong. No, it's common to have some repeated waves of fear and anxiety. Repeat as needed!

End

The E is there to remind you that these feelings will end, and so will the flight. It's easy to feel like time is standing still when you're afraid, facing thousands of years of fear without end. But, no. Every panic attack ends regardless of what the person does. If you respond in the most cogent way possible, the attack will end. If you respond in the most unhelpful way possible, taking the bait and really feeding into the fear, that will end as well. So, it's not up to you to bring the fear to an end. That will happen no matter what you do.

Your job is much more modest. Your job is to allow yourself to feel afraid on the plane, and give it time to pass. It will pass, no matter what you do. And if you're unsure of that, review your own history with fear. Have you ever had a fear, or a panic attack, that didn't end? You probably had some that lasted longer than you wished, but they all ended eventually.

That's how you can spend your time during the flight. Your fear will come and go, and you can practice observing it, responding in a neutral way, and giving it time to pass.

Assuming you're doing a round trip on the same day, you'll have some time in between flights for a bathroom break, a call home, maybe a snack, or a souvenir. You can briefly review the experience with your companion, if you brought one. Naturally, you've probably already wondered what that period will be like, even before you've taken the first flight. Be aware of that, but don't get too involved in trying to guess or predict. Take it the way you find it at the time.

That's your guide for your first practice flight! If you were actually flying the plane, the guide would have to be longer and more comprehensive. But you'll be a passenger, and this will be sufficient for the role of passenger.

It's stressful working to undo this phobia and preparing your practice flight, right? I think you'll be glad you did when your world opens up to travel that's been so difficult, even impossible, with this phobia. But right now, it's tiresome. If you're feeling especially run down by the effort, you might want to add a little mindfulness meditation to your repertoire. Not for during the flight—stick with the AWARE steps on board—but in the days and weeks before the flight, just to give yourself a break and enhance your ability to observe your thoughts—the good, the bad, and the ugly—with more distance, maybe even compassion.

If you already have a meditation practice, do that! If you don't, and you want to experience one, here's where to find a recorded meditation I've prepared for the occasion: http://www.anxietycoach.com/carbonelldownload.html.

And now, if you're ready, let's talk about booking your practice flight.

CHAPTER 12

Time to Arrange Your Practice Flight

....

Now it's time to arrange your practice flight. This is not a test, or a kind of graduation flight in which you demonstrate that you have ceased to be afraid of flying. Not at all! This flight is for practice.

The airline doesn't need the practice. Neither does the crew. They get plenty of practice. The practice is for you to let yourself feel afraid and work with it, rather than against it.

How will such practice benefit you, or any other fearful flier? It will help because opposing and resisting the fear is what actually maintains it. What you resist, persists, and so your task is to resist less and accept more.

Booking Your Flight

What makes for a good practice flight? I suggest you start with a flight on a commercial airline that takes about an hour each way. Book the complete round trip for one day if you can. If you live in a major metropolitan area in the United States, you probably have plenty of convenient choices near your home. Elsewhere, you may have to travel some, presumably by car, to get to a suitable airport. If you're flying out of a smaller airport and can't do the round trip in a single day, then you'll have to stay overnight and return the next day.

Is it okay to start with a private plane rather than a commercial airline? If most of your intended flying will be on a private plane (say, you're a business executive who will mostly be flying on the company jet), then that might be a reasonable starting point. But most people are looking to fly on commercial airlines, and if that's your goal, it will be more useful to start with one. If your fears are principally of the Type 2 variety, fearful of feeling trapped on the plane, it will be hard to get good practice with that fear on a private plane, because you can always tell the pilot to cut the flight short if you want, and that would undo the effects of the practice.

The flight doesn't have to be exactly an hour. Sometimes, from Chicago, we've used Indianapolis as a destination when other flights weren't available. That's only about a 40-minute trip, and it's worked just as well as longer distances. We've also flown to some cities a little over one hour away. You want to have a flight that's long enough that you have enough time to get afraid, respond to it, and allow the feelings to settle down before you land.

Multipurpose Trips?

Sometimes people want to use this trip for two purposes—as a practice flight and also to travel to a meeting, a wedding, or some other event they plan to attend.

I recommend against this. I think it's best to make this trip for no purpose other than your practice. One big reason is that, if you have a business meeting to attend as part of this trip, or some social event, you're naturally going to feel reluctant to let yourself get as anxious as you can. You're likely to have thoughts about wanting to keep your anxiety within certain limits so it doesn't interfere with the other purposes of your trip.

That might sound good to you even now, keeping your anxiety within certain limits. But let's remember why you're planning this flight in the first place. It'll be much better to make this first trip for the sole purpose of getting practice with your fear.

This is pretty counterintuitive, to deliberately seek out fear. It doesn't come naturally. But that's the point of the practice flight. Your mission is to plan a flight that will give you practice with feeling afraid in order to help your amygdala develop a new view of flying.

What About Medications?

This brings up a lot of questions. If you've been using anxiety medication, one of the benzodiazepines, should you take it before the flight? Or keep it handy in case you feel you need it? How about a glass of wine or a beer, is that okay, either before or during the flight?

Remember why you're taking this flight. You're taking this flight so you get the chance to feel afraid and respond differently. It would be a shame, after going through this work and expense, if you short-circuited the process that way. You wouldn't get as much out of it!

Benzodiazepines and alcohol will have the effect of lowering your anxiety, so I suggest you refrain from using either the day of your practice flight. If you're taking other medications for anxiety, SSRI antidepressants or similar medications that you take on a daily basis for an extended period of time, this is a little more complicated. If these medications have the effect of preventing you from experiencing panic attacks, then it will probably be necessary for you to wean down on them before you take a practice flight, because otherwise you might not be able to feel the fear you need during this flight. This is something to discuss with your prescribing doctor and therapist, if you have one. Don't simply stop taking this kind of medication without a plan that you develop with your doctor.

Travel Without Safety Behaviors

And what about the other kinds of safety behaviors you've come to use? Bringing movies, books, or games to distract yourself with? The good luck charm from your grandson? Wearing your lucky shirt? Closing your eyes? Grabbing the armrest? Emotional support animals?

Take another look at your list of safety behaviors and objects from Chapter 6. As you think about taking a flight without any of your safety behaviors, does it bring any new ones to mind? Are there other safety behaviors and objects that didn't make it onto your list? If so, add them now.

Keep in mind why you're taking this flight. The purpose is to get afraid and practice with those feelings. If you rely on these kinds of safety behaviors, it increases the chance that you'll come away from the flight thinking that these behaviors saved you from a terrible fate, and you won't feel any more willing to fly than before. This is the "response prevention" part of exposure; leave the safety behaviors and objects at home!

Items to Bring

Bring:

- This book

- A single 3 x 5 card on which you've written a couple of key phrases that you've found particularly helpful. One that people commonly use is: "Is it danger or discomfort?" Or, you might want to have a quick summary of the AWARE steps (from Chapter 11) there. If writing on a card is too retrograde for you, you can put it on your phone or digital device, but be aware of the restrictions on the use of phones and laptops.

- Several copies of the Panic Journal (in the appendix, as many as you think you might need)

- A couple of pens

- Tissues (because crying is allowed)

- Your boarding passes and photo ID, of course

- Two Graph sheets for use in tracking your anxiety level during the flights (find this in the appendix)

- A copy of the AWARE steps (find this in the appendix)

- A Panic Journal for use in observing and writing about your moments of high fear and panic (make the copies you think you'll need; find this in the appendix)

- Symptom Inventory Form (find this in the appendix)

- Two blank lined pages for additional journaling of your experience (find this in the appendix)

Travel Solo or with a Support Person?

Should you bring a support person with you? If you feel willing and able to take the flight by yourself, that's probably the best. Don't bring a support person if you feel you can manage on your own.

However, there are many people who would have a really hard time doing this first practice flight by themselves. If that's the case for you, bringing a support person might be a reasonable compromise to make, provided you know someone who can come and play a helpful role. What you don't want is to bring someone who will make decisions for you, reassure you, distract you, and act as your protector and manager. The ideal role for a support person to play is just to accompany you, listen to what you have to say, remind you that you have a plan, and leave all the decisions to you.

Think about who among your friends and family is firmly in your corner, who has your best interests at heart, and who is also able to stay separate and independent enough for you to work through the fear and anxiety on your own. This person won't necessarily be the closest family member. Sometimes family members are too close to you to allow you the independence and self-reliance that can make this trip a success. Sometimes family members want to help by sparing you any pain or discomfort, interfering with the work of exposure.

If your spouse or sibling finds it so hard to see you suffer and struggle that they will interfere with that and intervene to reduce your anxiety, then pick someone else. In a similar way, someone who thinks you should just get over it by toughing it out or by simply not thinking of it is probably too opinionated to be a good support companion.

This isn't a choice based on who loves you the most, or who you love the most. It is important that you freely pick the person who you believe can fulfill this role in the most useful way.

Your support companion should have read, or at least skimmed, this book, so they have some understanding of the purpose of this trip and how you are supposed to do this kind of exposure. I suggest that you read this chapter and Chapter 11 together, or at least discuss that material. The part that's usually hardest for them to understand is that it's not their job to calm you down or reassure you that all will be well. They should not try to manage the flight for you or be in charge of anything. Instead, they need to just go along for the ride and support your intention to practice feeling afraid and accepting the symptoms.

For the most part, your support companion should just sit silently with you. He shouldn't be asking "how do you feel?" every few minutes. He should remind you that you have responses and techniques to use when you get anxious. He should play a secondary role, initiating little or nothing, just responding to your requests and comments. Your companion should not, for example, decide to hold your hand because you look so nervous. However, your companion should allow you to hold his hand if that's what you choose to do.

For the outbound flight, I suggest he just sit there without reading or any other distractions, so it's clear to you that you can have his attention any time you need. On the return flight, it would be okay to relax this so that he can read a book or magazine, as long as you feel better about the return flight.

What should you be saying to your support companion? I suggest you periodically update her about your fear level based on the 100-point scale in your graphs and panic journals. If you feel particularly panicky, you can tell her that.

Support companions should respond to your saying how anxious you are, not by telling you that everything will be okay, but by reminding you that you have prepared some steps for responding to fear and anxiety, and asking if you want to do them now. They shouldn't be initiating anything on their own, just responding to what you choose to tell them. A good support companion will play second fiddle and never take charge.

If your companion sees that you breathing in an uncomfortable or anxious way, it would generally be okay for him to say something like, "Your breathing looks a little uncomfortable. Do you want to do the deep breathing exercise?" They should do the same thing if you mention that you're having trouble with your breathing. They should be reminding you to do the things you already know how to do, not trying to teach you something new.

If you should feel really anxious and say, "I'm so afraid!" it would be good for your companion to say something like, "I know it's scary for you. It's good you're working with this. Do you want to fill out a Panic Journal?" or "Do you want to use your AWARE steps?"

In each case, your companion should respond in a concrete way, acknowledging that you feel afraid, that they know this is why you're here, and reminding you of some of the steps in this book that you can use. Your companion needn't feel expert in these techniques and can also say, "Are there steps in the book that you want to use now?"

And, if you should say to your companion, "Why on earth did I come here?" she should remind you, "These miserable feelings, to practice with them, this is why you came here!"

Talking with Friends and Family

When your family and friends learn you've taken your first practice flight, or even that you've booked one, they're likely to be enthused, cheer your progress, and want to schedule a trip to Australia or some other far-off destination. They'll figure you're "cured," and take that as the signal to book all the trips they ever wanted to take with you.

It'll be important to set them straight on this. Even before your first practice flight, let them know that this is a process, not a cure, and that it will take you some time. Let them know that it's important for you, not them, to set your agenda and determine how rapidly you move on to fly greater distances. Tell them you're committed to solving this problem, and that you look forward to making those trips with them (if that's true), but that you have to make the decisions about scheduling future trips in ways that will foster your recovery.

And that's the right word for this process, recovery. This is not a cure for fear of flying. Cure is not the right word because the fear of flying is not a disease. It's an overgrown version of ordinary fear and anxiety that needs to be whittled down and retrained, not cured.

It's very common for loved ones, in their enthusiasm and lack of understanding of the fine points about your fear, to try to encourage you, and celebrate, in ways that feel like pressure. Don't hesitate to push back and explain the program to them. Educate them about what you're doing and how they can best be supportive.

That's the plan. Schedule a flight of about one hour for the purpose of practicing with feeling afraid and not taking the bait to struggle and resist the feelings. Leave at home the various objects and medications you might have been using in the past to ward off the anxiety. Use the self-observational tools in the appendix. If you bring a support companion, make sure that person is aware of the methods described in this book and prepared to play a passive supporting role.

Have a good, nervous flight!

CHAPTER 13

And Beyond...

· ·

You have a fear of flying that you want to overcome, because it detracts from the quality and freedom of your life rather than keeps you safe. It's an exaggerated fear that whispers rumors and outlandish threats that it's never delivered upon. When you try not to be afraid, your efforts to calm down all too often make your fear more severe and persistent. Your best path to reducing anxiety and fear, and regaining your ability to fly, is to get enough practice with feeling afraid that the fear becomes a smaller and smaller problem.

How long will this take? As you might expect, results will vary based on individual circumstances. What I recommend to people who complete my workshop is that they continue to fly after the workshop is over at least once every three months for at least one year. I recommend that they add some additional difficulty or characteristic each time to raise the level of the anxiety practice. This might mean taking a longer flight; flying at night, if that's something the person fears; flying without a companion, if that seems scary; flying over water; flying on an unfamiliar airline; sitting in a less comfortable location; and/or any other variable that might provide additional anxiety with which to practice. Over time, get practice with all the variables that have been bothering you.

Almost everyone who has attended my program completes the initial practice flight, and the overwhelming majority of those go on to fly in the manner I suggest for the following year.

This is sufficient practice for most people to get to the point where they can fly whenever it suits their purposes. They don't necessarily enjoy flying, nor are they always completely free of anxiety about it, but it becomes a manageable problem for them. Flying is a means to an end, and they can use it that way. Flying used to be the biggest part of the trip, from their perspective. Now it's the least important.

For most people, this is a problem that can be largely resolved with a year of effort. But speed is not what's most important. Moving in the right direction is what's most important. If you're moving in the wrong direction you're not going to get where you want, no matter how long you work at it. So long as you're moving in the right direction, you're quite likely to get what you want.

With the fear of flying, the right direction is to move right toward the anxiety and get sufficient practice with it so the fear fades away over time. The best way around it is through it.

Each year I get postcards from cities all around the globe. They come from Moscow and Paris and London and Madrid, and also from Miami and Nashville and Denver and Portland. On the flip side of the cityscapes and other pictures is usually a heartfelt message of thanks from a former phobic who is now free to move about the country, and the world.

I hope someday to get one from you!

Appendix

....

AWARE Steps

(For a more detailed explanation of the AWARE steps, see page 99)

A: ACKNOWLEDGE & ACCEPT

I observe my symptoms of fear and work with them. I don't try to ignore, deny, fight, or flee them.

W: WAIT & WATCH

I'm just a passenger. I observe and journal my thoughts and reactions while I wait to arrive at my destination.

A: ACT

I don't need to make the fear stop. That will happen no matter what I do. I just need to wait. If I can make myself more comfortable while waiting for the fear to pass, maybe with deep breathing or journaling, I can also do that.

R: REPEAT

When I experience repeated flurries of fear, I'll just take these steps from the top.

E: END

The fear will end even when I think it won't. All I need to do is wait, because I'm a passenger, not a pilot.

Outbound Flight

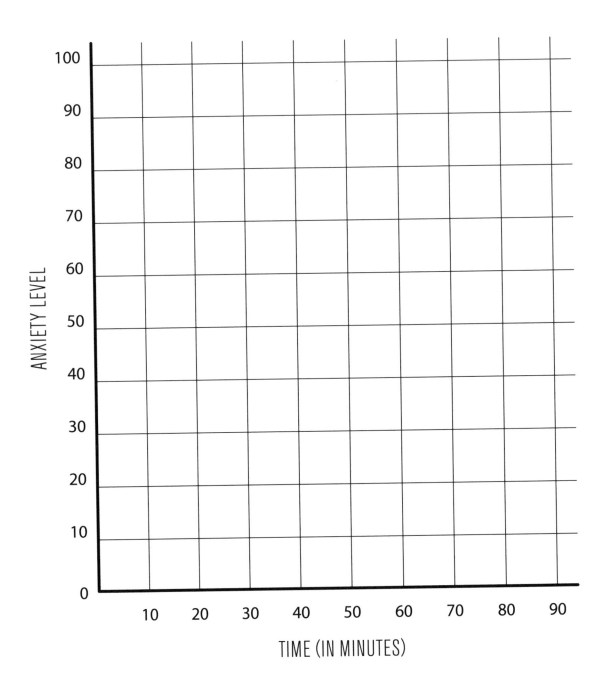

ANXIETY LEVEL

TIME (IN MINUTES)

Return Flight

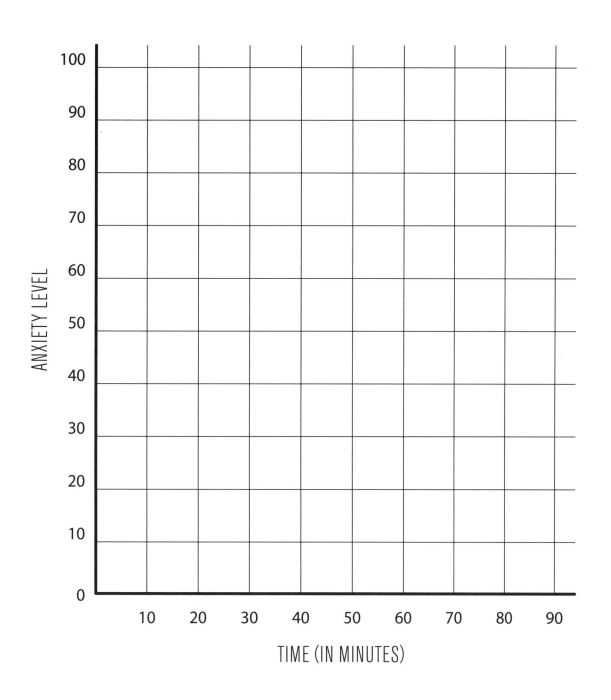

Outbound Flight

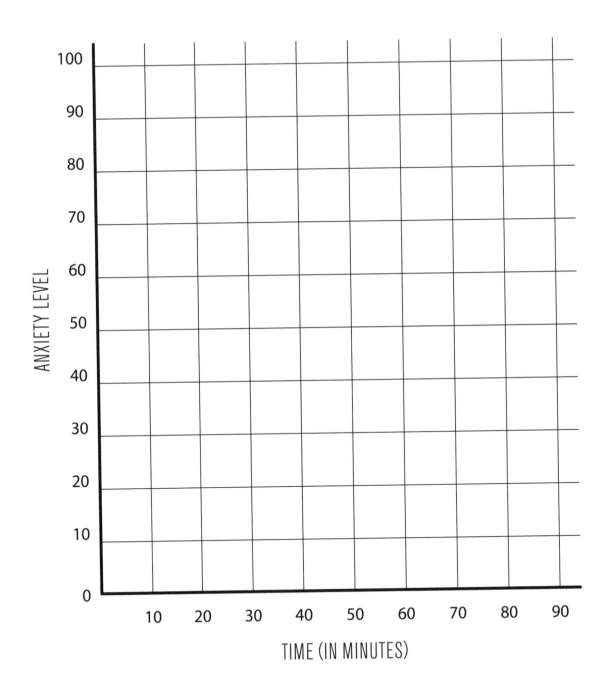

ANXIETY LEVEL

TIME (IN MINUTES)

Return Flight

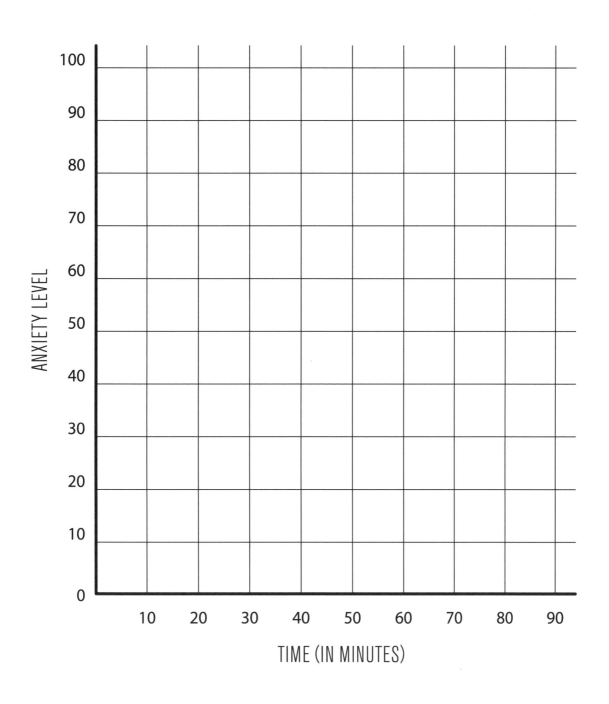

Symptom Inventory, Outbound Flight

Physical Sensations:

_____ ❑❑❑❑❑❑❑❑❑❑

_____ ❑❑❑❑❑❑❑❑❑❑

_____ ❑❑❑❑❑❑❑❑❑❑

_____ ❑❑❑❑❑❑❑❑❑❑

Thoughts:

_____ ❑❑❑❑❑❑❑❑❑❑

_____ ❑❑❑❑❑❑❑❑❑❑

_____ ❑❑❑❑❑❑❑❑❑❑

_____ ❑❑❑❑❑❑❑❑❑❑

Emotions:

_____ ❑❑❑❑❑❑❑❑❑❑

_____ ❑❑❑❑❑❑❑❑❑❑

_____ ❑❑❑❑❑❑❑❑❑❑

_____ ❑❑❑❑❑❑❑❑❑❑

Behaviors:

_____ ❑❑❑❑❑❑❑❑❑❑

_____ ❑❑❑❑❑❑❑❑❑❑

_____ ❑❑❑❑❑❑❑❑❑❑

_____ ❑❑❑❑❑❑❑❑❑❑

Symptom Inventory, Return Flight

Physical Sensations:

_____ ❑❑❑❑❑❑❑❑❑

_____ ❑❑❑❑❑❑❑❑❑

_____ ❑❑❑❑❑❑❑❑❑

_____ ❑❑❑❑❑❑❑❑❑

Thoughts:

_____ ❑❑❑❑❑❑❑❑❑

_____ ❑❑❑❑❑❑❑❑❑

_____ ❑❑❑❑❑❑❑❑❑

_____ ❑❑❑❑❑❑❑❑❑

Emotions:

_____ ❑❑❑❑❑❑❑❑❑

_____ ❑❑❑❑❑❑❑❑❑

_____ ❑❑❑❑❑❑❑❑❑

_____ ❑❑❑❑❑❑❑❑❑

Behaviors:

_____ ❑❑❑❑❑❑❑❑❑

_____ ❑❑❑❑❑❑❑❑❑

_____ ❑❑❑❑❑❑❑❑❑

_____ ❑❑❑❑❑❑❑❑❑

Panic Journal

Panic Level (0-100): _____   Time at start: _____   Time at end: _____

Physical Symptoms: _____

_____

_____

What were you thinking just before your anxiety increased? _____

_____

_____

_____

What were you reacting to? _____

_____

_____

_____

What scary thoughts are you having now? _____

_____

_____

_____

How are you responding to them?

____ distraction   ____ humor   ____ charting   ____ discussion with others

What are you saying to your scary thoughts? _____

_____

_____

_____

What are you doing to make yourself more comfortable physically?

____ deep breathing   ____ stretching   ____ getting up and standing   ____ walking

relaxing muscles of: ____ chest   ____ diaphragm   ____ throat   ____ shoulders   ____ jaw

What works best for you? List, in order. _____

_____

_____

_____

Notes

_____

_____

_____

_____

_____

_____

_____

_____

_____

_____

_____

_____

_____

_____

_____

_____

_____

_____

_____

_____

Notes

About the Author

....

David Carbonell, Ph.D., is a clinical psychologist who specializes in treating fears and phobias. He is the author of *Panic Attacks Workbook* and *The Worry Trick*, is the "coach" at the popular self-help site AnxietyCoach.com, and has taught workshops on the treatment of anxiety disorders to more than 7,000 professional psychotherapists in the United States and abroad. He received his doctorate in clinical psychology from DePaul University in 1985 and has maintained a practice in the treatment of anxiety disorders since 1990. He lives in Chicago with his wife and son. In his spare time, he is the founding member of The Therapy Players, an improvisational comedy troupe of professional psychotherapists that performs at clubs, theaters, and mental health conferences throughout the Chicago area.